Marie-Line André
de PurPle Laines

MANDALAS
& DOILIES
to crochet

Delightful Designs to Brighten Your Life

First published in the United States of America
in 2016 by
Trafalgar Square Books
North Pomfret, Vermont 05053

Originally published in French as *20 napperons et mandalas au crochet*.

Copyright © 2015 Marie-Line André and Éditions Mango
English translation © 2016 Trafalgar Square Books

ISBN: 978-1-57076-789-0

Library of Congress Control Number: 2016946076

Editorial director: Tatiana Delesalle
Editor: Marylise Trioreau
Artistic director: Chloé Eve
Photographer: Fabrice Besse
Stylist: Sonia Roy
Diagrams: Marie Pieroni
Project construction: Sabine Marioni
Translator: Elizabeth Gray

Printed in China

10 9 8 7 6 5 4 3 2 1

FOREWORD

Jacques Brel once said, "I wish you endless dreams, and the furious desire to realize them." Well, these were my dreams: to learn how to crochet, and to write a book.

When I was eight, I started to "work in the round," just winding pieces of wool I'd found around each other in a spiral. Later years brought the desire to always live in a world full of color. It's important to me to be able to create a certain atmosphere in my own space. Certain colors, for me, evoke specific styles or eras in art and design: natural colors are an invitation to minimalism and the spirit of Zen; bright colors bring back the post-war period of euphoria; oranges remind me of the seventies; pastel shades make everything feel like springtime; a splash of neon is like the crowing of a rooster first thing in the morning ... I love all of these sensations, all of these approaches. And it's worth taking the time to pick materials and colors that work together harmoniously, and to make things with them that suit whatever feel they create.

The doilies and mandalas in this book are an expression of my desire to share these combinations and sensations with you, so you can in your turn crochet yourself a world full of color.

My best wishes to all crocheters: may your head spin in the best way as you travel down these spiraling roads of color!

Marie-Line André

CONTENTS

GUIDE TO CROCHET

Holding the yarn and the hook

1. Place the yarn ball to your left. Lay the yarn across your left hand so the tail lies in your palm; the yarn should wrap around the back of your index finger, return to your palm across the base of your middle and ring fingers, and then pass between your ring finger and little finger to the back of your hand again.

2. Hold the yarn tail between your left thumb and middle finger. Hold the hook in your right hand, between your right thumb and index finger, an inch or two from the hook end.

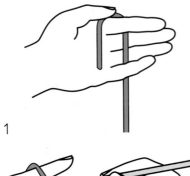
1

2

Crocheting in the round

All the patterns in this book are crocheted in the round. This means you'll always see the same side of the work (the right side), and you'll progress around the work counterclockwise.

It's a good idea to place a stitch marker to remind yourself where the beginning of the round is. Place the marker in the first stitch of the first round, and then move it up to the first stitch of each following round as you go. You can use additional stitch markers to help you keep track of increases, the positions of motifs, stitches you want to work over again later with overlay ... If you don't want to buy stitch markers, you can always use small pieces of scrap yarn instead—just slide one between two stitches and tie it loosely into a loop.

To keep your work in the round as circular as possible, it can be a good idea to stagger the beginnings of rounds a stitch or two instead of stacking them up right on top of each other. Each time you have to change colors, try making the join slightly to one side of the exact beginning of the round. Staggered like this, the beginnings and ends of rounds are less visible when the work is finished, and the increases are a little better distributed.

Charts

The pattern instructions are accompanied by charts, which let you visualize what you need to do very quickly. They aren't a realistic image of the exact placement and appearance of actual crocheting, but if you follow them while working, everything should come out correctly.

Follow these charts from the center out, and remember that rounds are worked counterclockwise.

Tip
If you're lefthanded, reverse the positions of the hands. You can photocopy the illustrations and look at them in a mirror to help you visualize how your hands should be held and how the yarn should be positioned.

Slipknot

To begin a piece of crochet, you need to start with a slipknot, which then is looped around the hook.

1. Form the yarn tail into a loop, with the tail passing under the end of the yarn that continues to the yarn ball (the "working yarn"). Put the crochet hook through the loop.

2. Hold the loop in place by pinching it between your left thumb and middle finger. With the hook, catch the working yarn and pull it toward you through the loop.

3. Pull on the yarn tail while holding the working yarn to tighten the loop into a knot. The working yarn you pulled through the loop now forms a loop around the hook that can be tightened by tugging a little on the working yarn. This is the loop you'll use to begin your crocheting.

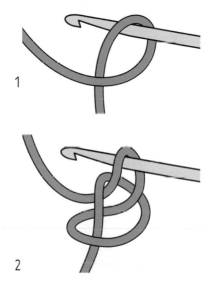

Chain stitch (ch)

Wrap the yarn around the hook from front to back (this is a yarnover, abbreviated "yo"). Pull this wrapped yarn through the loop on the hook: you have just worked a chain stitch.

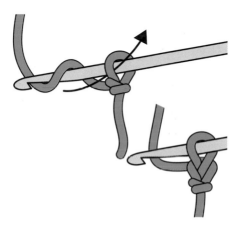

CHAIN

Multiple chain stitches in a row form a chain. A foundation chain is worked at the beginning of all crochet projects done in rows, and even some designs done in the round. It's important to note that the knot of the beginning slipknot and the loop on the hook don't qualify as chain stitches—when counting the number of stitches in a chain, don't include them.

RINGS OF CHAIN STITCHES

When you work with a foundation chain formed into a ring, don't work into the chain stitches—lower the hook into the ring and pull the working yarn through it and around the chain stitches, unless otherwise instructed in the pattern.

Slip stitch (sl st)

This stitch is useful for progressing along a row or round without adding much height to the work, and for joining the end of a round to the start of the next.

Insert the hook into the stitch of the previous row or round where a slip stitch is to be worked. Wrap the yarn around the hook. Pull the yarn through the stitch and then through the loop on the hook. You have worked one slip stitch and have a new loop on the hook.

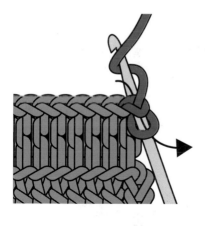

Working invisible slip stitch is explained on page 10.

Single crochet (sc)

1. Insert the hook into the stitch of the previous row or round where a single crochet is to be worked.

2. Wrap the yarn around the hook and pull through the stitch. There are now two loops on the hook.

3. Wrap the yarn around the hook again and pull through both loops. You have worked one single crochet stitch and have a new loop on the hook.

Half double crochet (hdc)

1. Wrap the yarn around the hook, and then insert the hook into the stitch of the previous row or round where a half double crochet is to be worked.

2. Wrap the yarn around the hook again and pull through the stitch. There are now three loops on the hook.

3. Wrap the yarn around the hook a third time and pull through all three loops on the hook. You have worked one half double crochet stitch and have a new loop on the hook.

Double crochet (dc)

1. Wrap the yarn around the hook, and then insert the hook into the stitch of the previous row or round where a double crochet is to be worked.

2. Wrap the yarn around the hook again and pull through the stitch. There are now three loops on the hook. Wrap the yarn around the hook a third time and pull it through two of those loops.

3. There are now two loops remaining on the hook. Wrap the yarn around the hook a fourth time and pull it through both loops. You have worked one double crochet stitch and have a new loop on the hook.

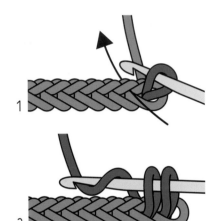

1

2

3

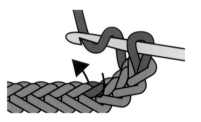

1

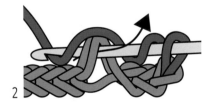

2

3

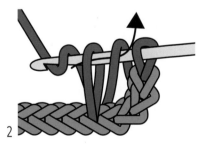

1

2

3

Double treble crochet (dtr)

Worked on the same principle as treble crochet, but with the yarn wrapped around the hook one more time at the beginning and one more time at the end.

1. Wrap the yarn around the hook three times, and then insert the hook into the stitch of the previous row or round where a double treble crochet is to be worked. Wrap the yarn around the hook again and pull through the stitch. There are now five loops on the hook.

2. Wrap the yarn around the hook and pull through two of the loops.

3. Repeat Step 2 twice. There are now two loops remaining on the hook.

4. Wrap the yarn around the hook one last time and pull it through both loops. You have worked one double treble crochet stitch and have a new loop on the hook.

Treble crochet (tr)

1. Wrap the yarn around the hook twice, and then insert the hook into the stitch of the previous row or round where a treble crochet is to be worked.

2. Wrap the yarn around the hook again and pull through the stitch. There are now four loops on the hook. Wrap the yarn around the hook once more annd pull it through two of these loops.

3. There are now three loops remaining on the hook. Wrap the yarn around the hook once more and pull it through two of these loops.

4. There are now two loops remaining on the hook. Wrap the yarn around the hook one last time and pull it through both loops. You have worked one treble crochet stitch and have a new loop on the hook.

Triple treble crochet (trtr)

Wrap the yarn around the hook four times; proceed as for the other treble crochet stitches, pulling through the stitch below and then two loops at a time until only one loop remains on the hook.

Quadruple treble crochet (quadtr)

Wrap the yarn around the hook five times; proceed as for the other treble crochet stitches, pulling through the stitch below and then two loops at a time until only one loop remains on the hook.

Additional stitches

It's possible to work stitches even taller than the quadruple treble crochet, following the same principles. Wrap the yarn around the hook the number of times indicated, and then proceed as for any of the treble crochets.

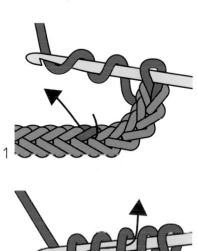

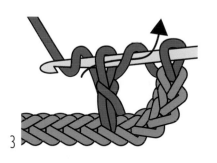

Working stitches together

Decreases are formed in crochet by working two or more incomplete stitches and then completing them simultaneously, as though they were a single stitch.

An incomplete stitch is worked up until the step before the last yarnover, and then the last two loops are simply left on the hook while another stitch is begun. The steps below describe working two double crochet stitches together (abbreviated "dc2tog").

1. Wrap the yarn around the hook and insert it into a stitch. Wrap the yarn around the hook again and pull through the stitch. Wrap the yarn around the hook a third time, and pull through just two of the loops on the hook = one incomplete double crochet stitch (two loops still left on the hook). Work a second incomplete double crochet in next stitch (three loops still left on the hook).

2. Wrap the yarn around the hook and pull through all three loops on hook.

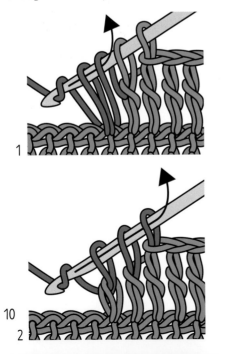

Standing stitches

Usually, when joining a new yarn anywhere along a row or round, it's standard to work a set number of chain stitches—this allows you to match the height the rest of the row will be, and takes the place of the first stitch to make joining easier. However, the patterns in this book use a different method: the standing stitch. The chain stitch method stands out a bit more obviously; standing stitches blend in better. The instructions below explain how to work a standing double crochet stitch, but the basic principle is the same for any standing stitch.

1. Wrap the yarn around the hook, from back to front, to create a loop on the hook (A). Wrap the yarn around the hook again to form the first additional loop for a double crochet (B).

2. Work the double crochet as usual, keeping the yarn tail in place with the right hand. Ensuring that the tail stays on the back of the work, pull on it gently to tighten the double crochet stitch and help keep it from coming undone. The tail can be woven in later.

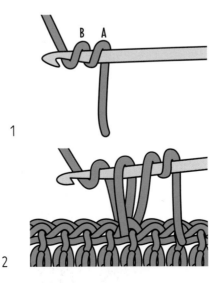

Fastening off

Cut the yarn about 4 in / 10 cm away from the work. Thread this tail onto a tapestry needle, pass it through the open loop from left to right, then pull gently to tighten and finish weaving in.

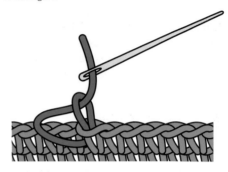

Invisible slip stitch

As the name implies, these blend in better than regular slip stitches. Use this method when you're at the end of a round and cutting the yarn. Unless otherwise indicated, an invisible slip stitch shouldn't be included in the overall stitch count.

1. Fasten off (see above).

2. Slide the tapestry needle under both sides of the first stitch of the round, from left to right, and then back through the open loop. Pull gently on the yarn tail to tighten, and then finish weaving in.

10

Front loop, back loop

No matter the stitch, unless otherwise indicated you should always work through both loops of the stitch below—they will form a horizontal V when you look down at the row from above.

To make ribbing, or when you'll be working back over some crocheting later with overlay crochet, some patterns will tell you to work through the front loop or back loop only.

Relief/raised crochet

Instead of inserting the crochet hook through the two loops that form the horizontal V at the top of the stitch, start at the front of the work and pass the hook around behind the "post" underneath them, from right to left, and then work the rest of the stitch as usual. This is a front post crochet stitch. You can also start at the back of the work and pass the hook forward around the post; this is a back post crochet stitch.

Overlay crochet

This technique consists of working into completed rows or rounds to create relief effects or to superimpose an additional pattern over what has already been worked. In these cases, overlay stitches can be worked like relief crochet stitches, or into the free loops of front-loop-only or back-loop-only sections of the work.

Changing yarn
STARTING A NEW YARN

Insert the hook into the stitch where you'd like to start a new yarn. Wrap the new yarn around the hook and pull through, and then continue as instructed.

CHANGING COLORS

Work the stitch right before the color change normally, up until the last pull-through; use the new color for that final step, and then continue as instructed in the new color (see adjacent diagram).

Multicolor crochet

To transition easily between colors that are both used at multiple points along the same row or round, and keep the thickness of the work consistent at the same time, it's a good idea to keep the unused yarn running along the back—or even inside the stitches being worked with the current yarn.

The principle remains the same with more than two yarns: all the unused yarns can be held inside the stitches being worked with the current yarn.

1. At the beginning of the row or round, hold the yarn that will be used for the patterning at the back of the work (Yarn B).

2. Begin crocheting with Yarn A, working the stitches around Yarn B so as to hide it inside them.

3. When you need to switch to Yarn B, swap it with Yarn A and keep crocheting, working the stitches in Yarn B around Yarn A.

Plan ahead for these color changes, and see the adjacent diagrams for guidance.

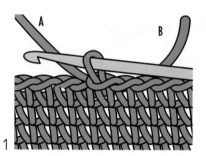

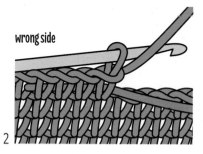

wrong side

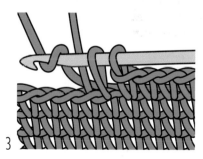

Magic ring

A piece of crocheting that will be worked in the round can be begun with a small foundation chain joined into a loop—or with a ring that can be tightened, which is typically called a "magic ring". The latter leaves a less obvious hole at the center of a work. The instructions below explain how to use a magic ring to start a work in single crochet, but the basic principle remains the same for any type of stitch.

1. Hold the yarn tail between the left thumb and left middle finger. Wrap the yarn twice around the left index finger.

2. Slide the resulting ring off the left index with the right hand, pinching it so it stays a ring.

3. Hold the ring between the left thumb and left middle finger, and extend the working yarn around the left index finger as usual. Insert the hook into the ring, wrap the yarn around the hook, and pull the yarn through the ring.

4. To work the chain stitch that begins the first round, wrap the yarn around the hook again and pull it through the loop on the hook.

5. Work the first single crochet stitch, inserting the hook into the ring instead of into a stitch.

6. When you've worked as many stitches as instructed, pull on the yarn tail left over from the ring to tighten it (depending on the effect you want, you can close the ring completely or leave a hole of whatever size you like in the center).

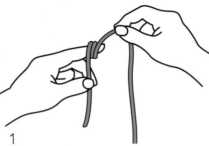

1

2

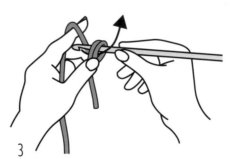

3

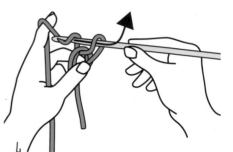

4

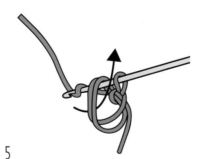

5

6

Yarn ends

Before the starting slipknot and at the end of a completed work, leave yourself yarn tails or ends that are long enough to be easily woven into the work. Do the same whenever you change colors or skeins in the middle of a work.

Weave in ends before blocking a completed work. You can use the hook to weave in ends, or you can thread them onto a tapestry needle. In either case, stay on the wrong side of work; weave them around and through several stitches on the same row or round, pull gently to make sure no loops of slack are left hanging out, and then trim the remainder.

Blocking

This is essential to help the work keep its final shape. Immerse the work fully in cold water and let it soak for about fifteen minutes. Then take it out of the water and press it flat—do not twist it or wring it out. Spread it on a towel, roll the towel up, and squeeze to remove excess water. Pin the work to a flat surface (such as a blocking mat), starting at the center and moving outward. If you have a drawing compass or similar, you can use that to make sure you have a perfect circle. Let dry for at least twenty-four hours (the time necessary to dry fully will be longer for multicolor patterns or patterns with overlay crochet).

If you want to stiffen the work, soak it in a mixture of equal parts water and powdered sugar. This method works well on cotton, but is not suitable for wool. You can also use fabric stiffener: once the work has been blocked and has dried, turn it over, pin it down again, and apply a thin layer of stiffener—sparingly, as this tends to darken the yarn colors.

Abbreviations

beg	begin, beginning
ch	chain
cl	cluster
cm	centimeter(s)
dc	double crochet (British: treble crochet)
dtr	double treble (British: triple treble)
gr	group
hdc	half double crochet (British: half treble crochet)
in	inch(es)
m	meter(s)
mm	millimeter(s)
pm	place marker
rem	remain(s)(ing)
rep	repeat
rnd(s)	round(s)
RS	right side
sc	single crochet (British: double crochet)
sl	slip
st(s)	stitch(es)
tr	treble (British: double treble)
trtr	triple treble (British: quadruple treble)
WS	wrong side
yd	yard(s)
yoh	yarn over hook, also yarn around hook

DECORATIVE MANDALAS AND DOILIES

instructions for Shaded Star on pages 26-27

instructions for Pastel Harmony on pages 28-31

instructions for Flower Tambourines on pages 36–41

instructions for Rudbeckia on pages 42-43

instructions for Pop! on pages 44–47

instructions for Dahlia on pages 48-49

instructions for Compass Rose on pages 50-53

instructions for Northern Lights on pages 54-55

instructions for Seventies on pages 56-59

SHADED STAR

photo on page 15

MATERIALS	Diameter after blocking: 12½ in / 31.5 cm	Difficulty: simple
DMC Six Strand Embroidery Floss (100% cotton; 9 yd/8 m per skein), 1 skein each of Indigo #336 (A), Dark Blue #312 (B), Pale Blue #775 (E), Light Blue #3325 (D); 2 skeins each of Medium Blue #334 (C), Cloud Blue #3756 (F), Edelweiss #3865 (G)	Crochet hook, U.S. B-1 / 2 mm For finishing: tapestry needle, scissors, basin of water, powdered sugar, blocking mat (or other surface), pins	

With Yarn A, ch 6. Join into a ring with 1 sl st into the 1st ch.

Rnd 1: Ch 4 (= 1 tr), 2 dc in ring, *1 tr in ring, 2 dc in ring*; rep * to * 4 more times and end with 1 sl st into the 4th ch = 18 sts.

Rnd 2: Ch 1 (= 1 sc), 1 sc at the base of this ch, 1 sc in each of next 2 dc, *2 sc in next tr, 1 sc in each of next 2 dc*; rep * to * 4 more times; with Yarn B, 1 sl st into the 1st ch = 24 sc. Cut Yarn A and continue with Yarn B.

Rnd 3: Ch 6 (= 1 sc + 1 ch loop), skip 3 sc, 1 sc in next sc, *ch 5 (= 1 ch loop), skip 3 sc, 1 sc in next sc*; rep * to * 4 more times, and end with 1 sl st into the 1st ch instead of 1 sc = 6 sc and 6 ch loops of 5 ch each.

Rnd 4: Ch 1 (= 1 sc); *[work 4 dc, 3 tr and 4 dc in next ch loop]; 1 sc in next sc*; rep * to * 4 more times, rep inside brackets once more; with Yarn C, 1 sl st into the 1st ch = 72 sts. Cut Yarn B and continue with Yarn C.

Rnd 5: Ch 1, *1 sc in each of next 11 st, 1 sl st into the next sc*; rep * to * 5 more times, ending with last sl st into the 1st ch.

Rnd 6: 1 sl st into each of first 6 sc; *[ch 15, skip last ch, 1 sl st into each of next 8 ch; ch 6], skip 10 sc, 1 sl st into next sc*; rep * to * 4 more times, rep inside brackets once more, and end with 1 sc between 5th and 6th sl sts = 6 groups of sl sts.

Rnd 7: *Ch 13, 1 sc in the ch at the far end of next group of sl sts, ch 13, 1 sc in next sl st*; rep * to * 5 more times, ending with 1 invisible sl st instead of 1 sc (you will need to cut yarn) in the final sc of Rnd 6 = 12 groups of 13 ch each.

Rnd 8: With Yarn C, 1 standing sc in the sc between ch groups, *ch 27, 1 sc in st between ch groups*; rep * to * 4 more times, ch 27; with Yarn D, 1 sl st into the standing sc. Cut Yarn C and continue with Yarn D.

Rnd 9: *Ch 9, skip 6 ch, 1 sc in next ch*; rep * to * around, ending with 1 sl st into the 1st ch instead of 1 sc = 24 sc and 24 ch loops of 9 ch each.

Rnd 10: 1 sl st into each of first 5 ch, *ch 9, 1 sc in next ch loop*; rep * to * around, ending with 1 invisible sl st instead of 1 sc (you will need to cut yarn) at the base of the first ch loop.

Rnd 11: With Yarn E, beg rnd with 1 standing sc in the middle of a ch loop. *ch 10, 1 sc in next ch loop*; rep * to * around, ending with 1 sl st into the standing sc instead of 1 sc.

Rnd 12: 1 sl st into each of first 5 ch, *ch 11, 1 sc in next ch loop*; rep * to * around, ending with 1 invisible sl st instead of 1 sc (you will need to cut yarn) at the base of the first ch loop.

Rnd 13: With Yarn F, beg rnd with 1 standing sc in the middle of a ch loop. *ch 12, 1 sc in next ch loop*; rep * to * around, ending with 1 sl st into the standing sc instead of 1 sc.

Rnd 14: 1 sl st into each of first 6 ch, *ch 13, 1 sc in next ch loop*; rep * to * around, ending with 1 invisible sl st instead of 1 sc (you will need to cut yarn) at the base of the first ch loop.

Rnd 15: With Yarn G, beg rnd with 1 standing sc in the middle of a ch loop. *ch 14, 1 sc in next ch loop*; rep * to * around, ending with 1 sl st into the standing sc instead of 1 sc.

Rnd 16: 1 sl st into each of first 7 ch, *ch 15, 1 sc in next ch loop*; rep * to * around, ending with 1 invisible sl st instead of 1 sc (you will need to cut yarn) at the base of the first ch loop.

Weave in ends. Soak the work for 20 minutes in a mixture of equal parts water and powdered sugar, and then block (see page 13).

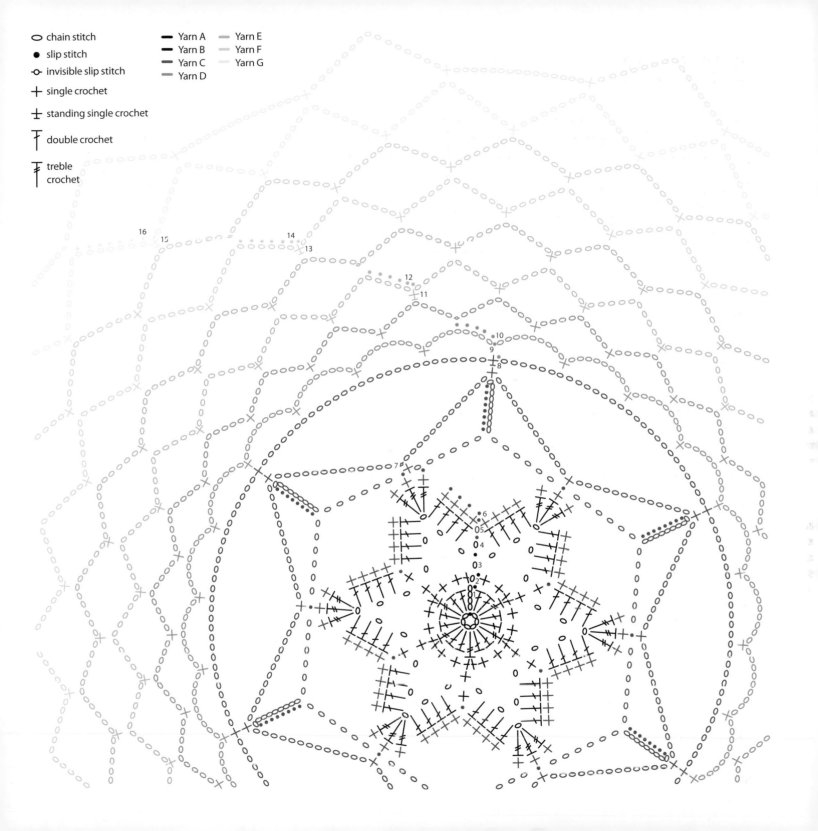

○ chain stitch
● slip stitch
-○- invisible slip stitch
+ single crochet
± standing single crochet
† double crochet
‡ treble crochet

— Yarn A   — Yarn E
— Yarn B   — Yarn F
— Yarn C   — Yarn G
— Yarn D

PASTEL HARMONY

photo page 16 - charts pages 30-31

MATERIALS	Diameter after blocking: 11 in / 28 cm	Difficulty: intermediate

CYCA #1 (sock/fingering/baby) DMC Natura Just Cotton (100% combed cotton; 170 yd/155 m / 50 g)	Crochet hook, U.S. size E-4 / 3.5 mm
50 g of each of the following: Sable N03 (A), Rose Layette N06 (B), Lobelia N82 (C), Light Green N12 (D), Gris Argent N09 (E)	Tapestry needle, pair of scissors, basin of water, blocking mat (or other surface), pins, drawing compass

PATTERN STITCH
"Nonuple" double crochet

Roll the yarn a little bit between your fingers so the ply is tight, and then wrap it around the hook 9 times. Insert the hook into a stitch, wrap the yarn around the hook, and pull through. *Wrap the yarn around the hook and pull through the first 2 loops on the hook*; rep * to * 9 times.

Note

The raised lines of crocheting are done using overlay crochet (see page 11). To leave room for the overlay crochet stitches later, Rnds 3-20 need to be worked through back loops only.

With Yarn A, make a magic ring.

Rnd 1: Ch 4 (= 1 tr); work 1 dc, 1 hdc and 1 dc into ring; *1 tr, 1 dc, 1 hdc, and 1 dc into ring*; rep * to * 4 more times, cut yarn, and end with 1 invisible sl st in the 3rd ch = 24 sts. Tighten ring.

Rnd 2: With Yarn B, work 1 standing sc and 2 sc into 1 tr, *[1 sc in next dc, skip 1 hdc, 1 sc in next dc], 3 sc in next tr*; rep * to * 4 more times, rep within brackets once more, cut yarn, and end with 1 invisible sl st in the standing sc = 30 sc.

Rnd 3: Begin with Yarn B and work into the center sc of a group of 3 sc from Rnd 2. *Ch 5, skip 4 sc, 1 sc in back loop only in next sc*; rep * to * 4 more times, ch 5, and end with 1 sl st into the standing sc = 6 sc and 6 ch loops.

Rnd 4: Ch 1, *7 sc around ch loop, 1 sc in back loop only in next sc*; rep * to * 5 more times, cut yarn, and end with 1 invisible sl st into 1st sc = 48 sc.

Rnd 5: With Yarn C, work 1 standing sc in back loop only; 1 sc in back loop only of each st around, cut yarn, and end with 1 invisible sl st in the standing sc.

Rnd 6: With Yarn D, work 1 standing sc in back loop only and 1 sc in back loop only in the same st. [*1 sc in back loop only in next sc, (2 sc in back loop only in next sc, 1 sc in back loop only in each of next 2 sc) two times *, 2 sc in back loop only in next sc]; rep within brackets 4 more times, rep * to * once more, cut yarn, and end with 1 invisible sl st in the standing sc = 66 sc.

Rnd 7: With Yarn B, work 1 standing sc into an sc from Rnd 6 that is vertically in line with the 3rd sc of a group of 7 sc from Rnd 4. *[Working into Rnd 4, dtr2tog in front loop only, with 1 dtr worked into the sc before a group of 7 sc and the other dtr worked into the sc after the same group; on Rnd 6, skip 1 sc], 1 sc in back loop only in each of next 10 sc*; rep * to * 4 more times, rep within brackets once more, 1 sc in back loop only in each of last 9

sc, cut yarn, and end with 1 invisible sl st in the standing sc = 66 sts, with 6 points of a star shape formed by the overlay crochet.

Rnd 8: Work as for Rnd 5.

Rnd 9: With Yarn D, work 1 standing sc in back loop only and 1 sc in back loop only in the same st, 1 sc in back loop only in next sc, *[2 sc in back loop only in next sc, 1 sc in back loop only in each of next 2 sc], rep within brackets 2 more times, 2 sc in back loop only in next sc, 1 sc in back loop only in next sc*; rep * to * 4 more times, rep within brackets 3 more times, cut yarn, and end with 1 invisible sl st in the standing sc = 90 sc.

Rnd 10: With Yarn A, work as for Rnd 5.

Rnd 11: With Yarn B, work 1 standing sc in back loop only and 1 sc in back loop only in the same st, 1 sc in back loop only in each of next 2 sc, *2 sc in back loop only in next sc, 1 sc in back loop only in each of next 2 sc*; rep * to * around, cut yarn, and end with 1 invisible sl st in the standing sc = 120 sc.

Rnd 12: Locate an sc vertically in line with one of the sc from Rnd 4 that has 2 dtr worked in its front loop. With Yarn A, work 1 standing sc in back loop only in the sc *before* that sc; *[working into Rnd 10, 2 dc in front loop only into next sc; skip 2 sc of Rnd 11], 1 sc in back loop only in each of next 18 sc*; rep * to * 4 more times, rep within brackets once more, 1 sc in back loop only in each of last 17 sc, cut yarn, and end with 1 invisible sl st in the standing sc = 120 sts.

Rnd 13: With Yarn D, work 1 standing sc in back loop only into an sc several sts away from any of the dc of Rnd 12. *1 sc in back loop only into each of next several sts until you are 1 st away from a dc; [working into Rnd 9, 1 tr in front loop only in the sc beneath the sc of Rnd 10 with 2 dc worked into its front loop; skip 1 sc of Rnd 12], 1 sc in back loop only in each of next 2 dc, rep within brackets once more*; rep * to * 5 more times, 1 sc in back loop only in each sc rem, cut yarn, and end with 1 invisible sl st in the standing sc.

Rnd 14: With Yarn C, work 1 standing sc in back loop only into an sc several sts in front of the tr of Rnd 13. *1 sc in back loop only into each of next several sts until you are 1 st away from a tr; [working into Rnd 8, 1 dtr in front loop only in the sc beneath the sc of Rnd 9 with 2 tr worked into its front loop; skip 1 sc of Rnd 13], 1 sc in back loop only in each of next 4 sts, rep within brackets once more*; rep * to * 5 more times, 1 sc in back loop only in each sc rem, cut yarn, and end with 1 invisible sl st in the standing sc.

Rnd 15: With Yarn A, work 1 standing sc in back loop only of the 1st dtr of a pair of dtr, 1 sc in back loop only in next sc. *[Working into Rnd 12, dc2tog in front loop only over the matching dc below; skip 2 sc of Rnd 14], 1 sc in back loop only in each of next 18 sts*; rep * to * 4 more times, rep within brackets once more, 1 sc in each sc rem, cut yarn, and end with 1 invisible sl st in the standing sc = 114 sts.

Rnd 16: With Yarn D, work 1 standing sc in back loop only into an sc several sts away from any of the dc worked tog in Rnd 15. *1 sc in back loop only into each of next several sts until you are 1 st away from 2 dc worked tog; working into Rnd 13, tr2tog in front loop only over the matching tr below; skip 1 st of Rnd 15*; rep * to * 5 more times, 1 sc in back loop only in each sc rem, cut yarn, and end with 1 invisible sl st in the standing sc.

Rnd 17: With Yarn C, work 1 standing sc in back loop only into an sc several sts away from any of the tr worked tog in Rnd 16. *1 sc in back loop only into each of next several sts until you've reached 2 tr worked tog; working into Rnd 14, tr2tog in front loop only over the dtr below; skip 1 st of Rnd 16*; rep * to * 5 more times, 1 sc in back loop only in each sc rem, cut yarn, and end with 1 invisible sl st in the standing sc.

Rnd 18: With Yarn B, work 1 standing sc in back loop only in the sc before 2 tr worked tog in Rnd 17. *[2 sc in back loop only into the tr2tog, 1 sc in back loop only in each of next 8 sc; work 1 nonuple dc into front loop of dtr2tog from Rnd 7 and around the loop between them; skip 1 sc of Rnd 17], 1 sc in back loop only in each of next 9 sc*; rep * to * 4 more times, rep within brackets once more, 1 sc in back loop only in each sc rem, cut yarn, and end with 1 invisible sl st in the standing sc = 120 sts.

Rnd 19: With Yarn E, work 1 standing sc in back loop only of a st, *[2 sc in back loop only in next st], 1 sc in back loop only in each of next 5 sts*; rep * to * around until 5 sts rem. Rep within brackets once more, 1 sc in back loop only in each st rem, cut yarn, and end with 1 invisible sl st in the standing sc = 140 sc.

Rnd 20: With Yarn A, work 1 standing tr in back loop only of a st; 1 tr in back loop only of prev st, with this tr passing behind the standing tr; *skip 1 sc, 1 tr in back loop only of next sc; 1 tr in back loop only of skipped sc, with this tr passing behind the prev tr*; rep * to * around, cut yarn, and end with 1 invisible sl st in the standing tr = 70 pairs of tr.

Rnd 21: With Yarn E, work 1 standing sc between 2 pairs of tr. *Ch 1, skip 1 tr, 1 sc between next pair of tr*; rep * to * around, cut yarn, and end with 1 invisible sl st (= 1 ch) in the standing sc = 140 sts.

Rnd 22: With Yarn B, 1 standing dc into an sc, *dc4tog in next ch, 1 dc in next sc*; rep * to * around until 1 ch rem—dc4tog in last ch, cut yarn, and end with 1 invisible sl st in the standing dc.

Rnd 23: With Yarn E, 1 standing sc into a dc, *ch 2, skip 1 group of 4 dc worked tog, 1 sc in next dc*; rep * to * around until last dc, ch 1, cut yarn, and end with 1 invisible sl st (= 1 ch) in the standing sc = 70 sc and 70 ch loops.

Rnd 24: With Yarn D, 1 standing sc around ch loop, *ch 2, 1 sc around next ch loop*; rep * to * around until last ch loop, ch 1, cut yarn, and end with 1 invisible sl st (= 1 ch) in the standing sc.

Rnd 25: With Yarn E, 1 standing sc around ch loop, ch 5, 1 sl st into the 1st ch, 1 sc around the same ch loop; around each of rem ch loops, work 1 sc, ch 5, 1 sl st into the 1st ch and 1 sc; cut yarn and end with 1 invisible sl st in the standing sc = 70 picots.

Weave in ends. Block work (see page 13): pin in place so the six-pointed star/flower shape of the first few rounds is accentuated. Make sure the work is nicely stretched, too, so the overlay crochet lies flat and nothing is loose or overlapping.

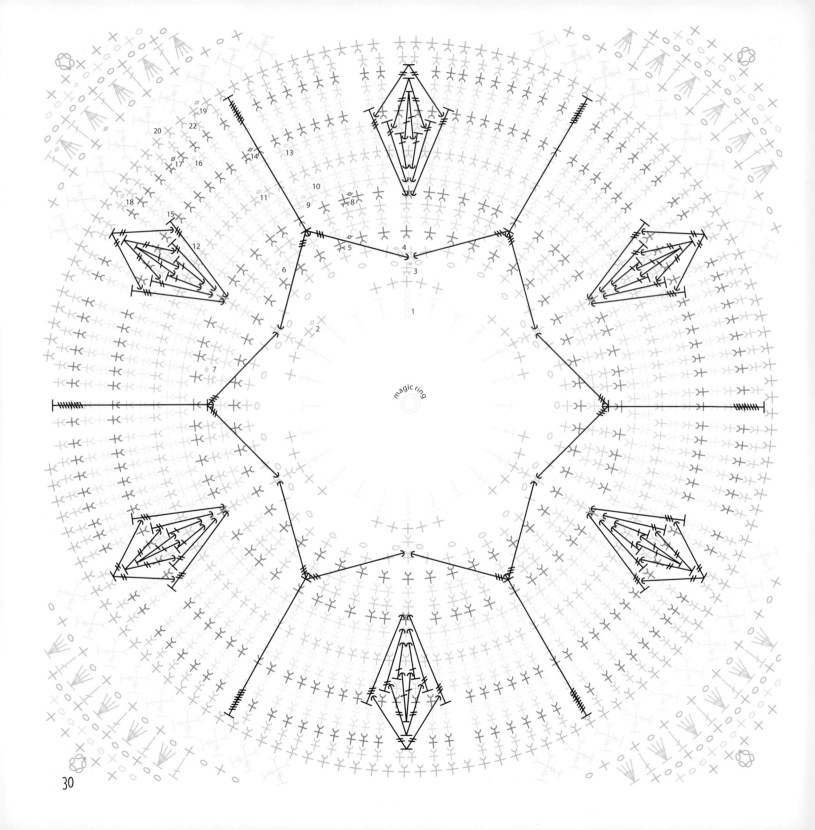

magic ring

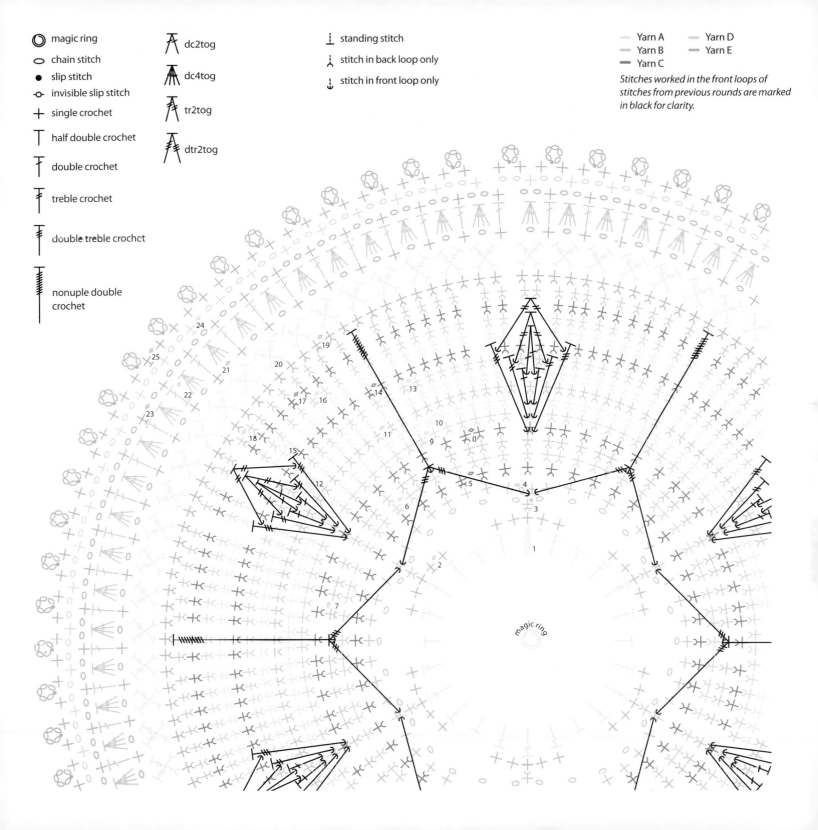

magic ring

chain stitch

slip stitch

invisible slip stitch

single crochet

half double crochet

double crochet

treble crochet

double treble crochet

nonuple double
crochet

dc2tog

dc4tog

tr2tog

dtr2tog

standing stitch

stitch in back loop only

stitch in front loop only

Yarn A   Yarn D

Yarn B   Yarn E

Yarn C

Stitches worked in the front loops of
stitches from previous rounds are marked
in black for clarity.

magic ring

SUMMERTIME FLOWER

photo page 17 - charts pages 34-35

MATERIALS	Diameter after blocking: 11¾ in / 30 cm	Difficulty: intermediate
CYCA #1 (sock/fingering/baby) DMC Natura Just Cotton (100% combed cotton; 170 yd/155 m / 50 g) 50 g of each of the following: Ibiza N01 (A), Golden Lemon N43 (B), Turquoise N49 (C), Erica N51 (D)	Crochet hook, U.S. size D-3 / 3 mm Tapestry needle, pair of scissors, basin of water, blocking mat (or other surface), pins, drawing compass	

PATTERN STITCH
7-dc bobble

Work 7 incomplete dc into the same stitch (see page 10, Working stitches together): you'll end up with 8 loops on the hook. Wrap the yarn around the hook and pull through all 8 loops at once.

With Yarn A, make a magic ring.

Rnd 1: Ch 3 (= 1 dc), 9 dc into ring, 1 sl st into 3rd ch = 10 dc. Tighten ring.

Rnd 2: Ch 5 (= 1 dc + 1 ch loop). *1 dc in next dc, ch 2*; rep * to * 7 more times, 1 dc in next dc, ch 1, cut yarn, and end with 1 invisible sl st in 3rd ch at beg of rnd = 10 dc and 10 ch loops.

Rnd 3: With Yarn B, work 1 standing sc into a dc, 2 sc into following ch loop. *1 sc in next dc, 2 sc into next ch loop*; rep * to * around, cut yarn, and end with 1 invisible sl st in the standing sc = 30 sc.

Rnd 4: With Yarn C, work 1 standing dc into an sc, *1 7-dc bobble in next sc, 1 dc into next sc*; rep * to * 13 more times, 1 7-dc bobble into last sc, cut yarn, and end with 1 invisible sl st in the standing dc = 15 bobbles (30 sts total).

Rnd 5: With Yarn B, work 1 standing sc into a dc, *2 sc in next bobble, 1 sc in next dc*; rep * to * around until 1 bobble rem, 2 sc in last bobble, cut yarn, and end with 1 invisible sl st (= 1 sc) in the standing sc = 46 sc.

Rnd 6: With Yarn A, work 1 standing dc into an sc, ch 1, *1 dc in next sc, ch 1*; rep * to * around and end with 1 sl st into the standing dc = 92 sts.

Rnd 7: Ch 3 (= 1 dc), skip 3 sts, 1 dc into next st, *ch 3; dc2tog with 3 skipped sts between dc = 1 incomplete dc in next st, skip 3 sts, 1 incomplete dc in next st, complete both dc at once*; rep * to * 3 more times, [ch 3; dc2tog with 2 skipped sts between dc]; rep * to * 5 more times, rep within brackets once more, rep * to * 6 more times, rep within brackets once more, ch 2, and end with 1 sl st into 3rd ch = 19 inverted Vs of dc2tog and 19 ch loops.

Rnd 8: Work 1 sl st into 1st inverted V, ch 3 (= 1 dc), *ch 1; into next ch loop, work [1 dc, ch 1], rep within brackets once; 1 dc into next inverted V*; rep * to * until 1 inverted V rem. Ch 1; into next ch loop, work 1 dc, ch 1 and 1 dc; cut yarn, and end with 1 invisible sl st (= 1 ch) in 3rd ch = 114 sts.

Rnd 9: With Yarn B, work 1 standing sc into dc, 1 sc in each of next 56 sts, skip 1 st, 1 sc in each of next 55 st, cut yarn, and end with 1 invisible sl st in the standing sc = 112 sc.

Rnd 10: With Yarn D, work 1 standing dc into an sc, *[ch 1, skip 1 sc, 1 7-dc bobble in next sc], ch 1, skip 1 sc, 1 dc into next sc*; rep * to * 26 more times, rep within brackets once more, cut yarn, and end with 1 invisible sl st (= 1 ch) in the standing dc = 112 sts, 28 7-dc bobbles.

Rnd 11: With Yarn B, work 1 standing sc into a dc, [*2 sc around next ch, 1 sc in next bobble, 2 sc around next ch, 1 sc in next dc*; rep * to * 5 more times, (2 sc around next ch, 1 sc in next bobble, 1 sc around next ch, 1 sc in next dc)]; rep within brackets 3 more times, ending last rep at 1 sc around next ch. Cut yarn and end with 1 invisible sl st in the standing sc = 164 sc.

Rnd 12: With Yarn C, work 1 standing sc into an sc, ch 1, *skip 1 sc, 1 sc into next sc, ch 1*; rep * to * around, cut yarn, and end with 1 invisible sl st in the standing sc = 164 sts.

Rnd 13: With Yarn A, work 1 standing sc around a ch, ch 1, *skip 1 sc, 1 sc in next ch, ch 1*; rep * to * around, cut yarn, and end with 1 invisible sl st in the standing sc.

Rnd 14: With Yarn D, work as for Rnd 13.

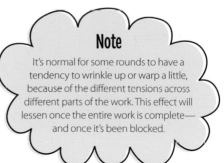

Rnd 15: Work as for Rnd 13.

Rnd 16: With Yarn C, work as for Rnd 13.

Rnd 17: With Yarn B, work 1 standing sc into any st and then sc around; cut yarn and end with 1 invisible sl st in the standing sc = 164 sc.

Rnd 18: With Yarn C, work as for Rnd 10: rep * to * 39 times = 41 7-dc bobbles (164 sts total).

Rnd 19: With Yarn B, work 1 standing sc into a dc, [*2 sc around next ch, 1 sc in next dc*; rep * to * once more, (2 sc around next ch, 1 sc in next bobble, 1 sc around next ch, 1 sc in next dc)]; rep within brackets 12 more times, rep * to * once more, and rep within parentheses once more, ending last rep with 1 sc around next ch. Cut yarn and end with 1 invisible sl st in the standing sc = 232 sc.

Rnd 20: With Yarn A, work 1 standing dc into an sc, *ch 1, skip 1 sc, 1 dc in next sc*; rep * to * around until last sc and end with 1 sl st into the standing dc – 232 sts.

Rnd 21: Ch 3 (= 1 dc), skip 2 sts, 1 dc in next st, *ch 2; dc2tog with 2 skipped sts between dc*; rep * to * around, ch 1, and end with 1 sl st into 3rd ch = 58 inverted Vs of dc2tog and 58 ch loops.

Rnd 22: 1 sl st into 1st inverted V, ch 3 (= 1 dc), *[ch 1, 1 dc around next ch loop, ch 1], 1 dc into next inverted V*; rep * to * around until last inverted V, rep within brackets once, and end with 1 sl st into 3rd ch = 232 sts.

Rnd 23: Ch 1; sc around, working sc2tog once at some point along the rnd, and end with 1 sl st into 1st sc = 231 sc.

Rnd 24: Ch 3 (= 1 dc), 1 sl st into 3rd sc (= 2 sc skipped between the base of the ch and the sl st), 5 dc at the base of the ch 3, skip 2 sc, 1 sl st into next sc, *1 sl st into next sc, skip 2 sc, 6 dc in next sc, skip 2 sc, 1 sl st into next sc*; rep * to * 31 more times, replacing last sl st with an invisible sl st (you will need to cut yarn) on last rep = 33 6-dc fans and 33 pairs of sl sts.

Rnd 25: With Yarn D, work 1 standing sc into 1st dc of a 6-dc fan, 1 sc into each of next 5 dc, *1 sc in next sl st, skip 1 sl st, 1 sc in each of next 6 dc*; rep * to * 31 more times, cut yarn, and end with 1 invisible sl st into next sl st = 231 sc.

Weave in ends. Block the work (see page 13). It's important to make the bobbles as prominent as possible when blocking—push them up from below so they all "pop out" to the right side.
It's also a good idea to take care with the shapes of the dc fans around the border of the piece: Place pins around each fan so they follow the same curve as the rest of the work, and add more pins as needed around the outer edge so the fans are stretched flat outwards.

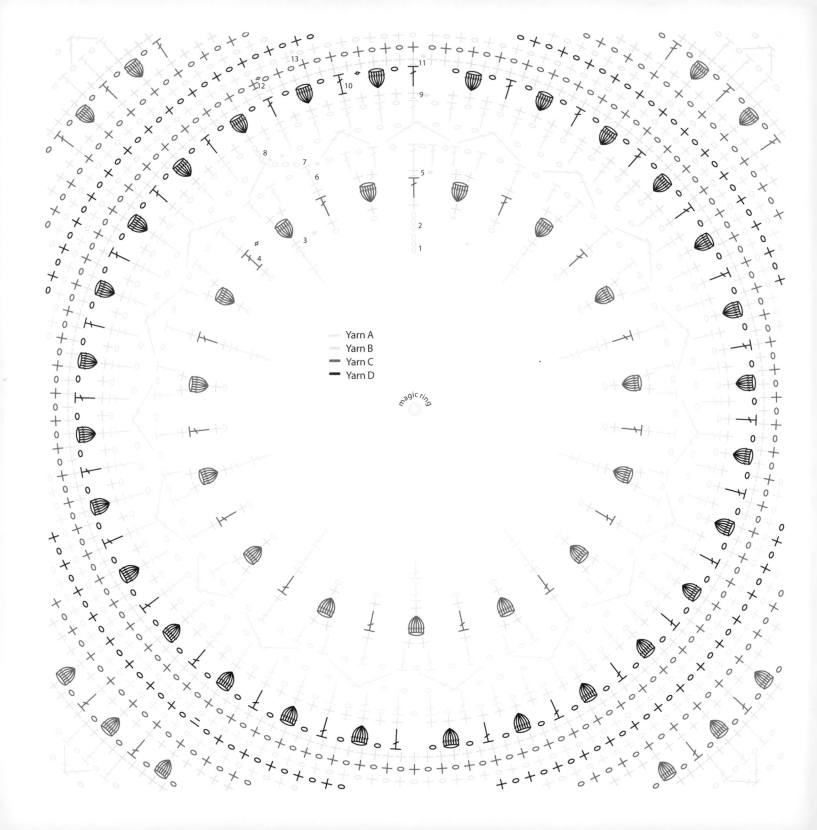

Yarn A
Yarn B
Yarn C
Yarn D

magic ring

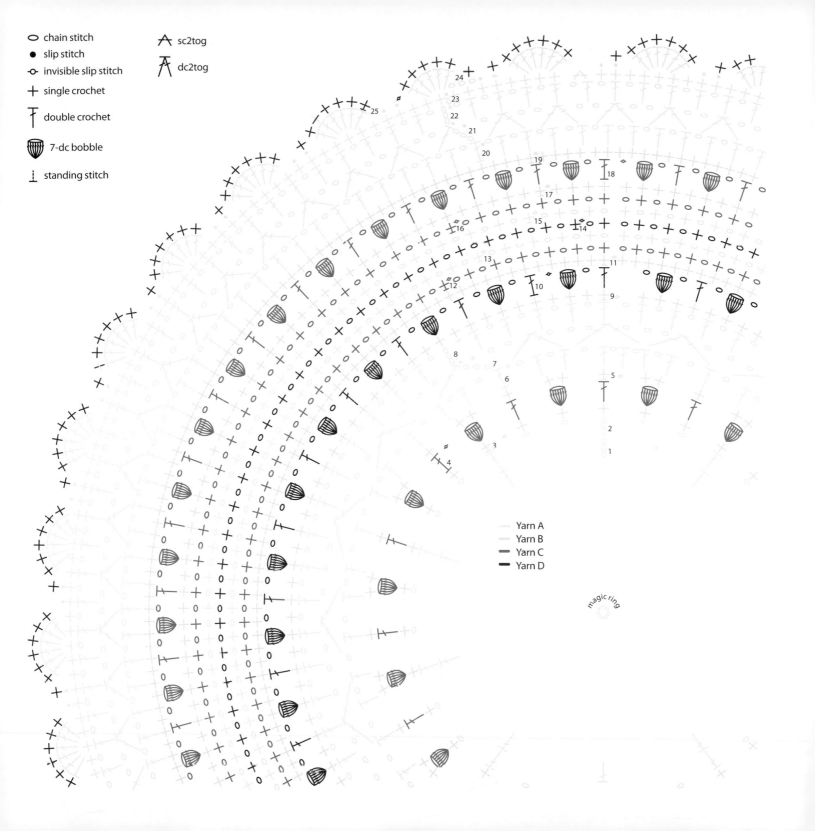

Key:

- ⬭ chain stitch
- ● slip stitch
- ⬯ invisible slip stitch
- + single crochet
- ⊤ double crochet
- 🛡 7-dc bobble
- ⊥ standing stitch

- ⋀ sc2tog
- ⋀̄ dc2tog

Yarn A
Yarn B
Yarn C
Yarn D

magic ring

LARGE FLOWER TAMBOURINE

photos pages 18-19 - chart pages 38-39

MATERIALS	Diameter: 8¼ in / 21 cm	Difficulty: simple
CYCA #3 (DK/light worsted) DMC Tapestry Wool Colbert (100% wool; 42 yd/38 m / 20 g), 20 g each of Mauve 7895 (A), Sky Blue 7599 (B), Pastel Pink 7132 (C), Lemon-Yellow 7431 (D), and Blue-Green 7296 (E)	1 embroidery hoop, 8¼ in / 21 cm in diameter Crochet hook, U.S. size G-6 / 4 mm Tapestry needle, pair of scissors, paint in pastel pink, paintbrush

Paint both parts of the embroidery hoop separately and let dry.

With Yarn A, make a magic ring.

Rnd 1: Ch 3 (= 1 dc), 1 dc into ring, ch 1, *2 dc, ch 1*; rep * to * 4 more times, replacing last ch with 1 invisible sl st into 3rd ch (you will need to cut yarn) on last rep = 6 pairs of dc and 6 ch between. Tighten ring.

Rnd 2: With Yarn B, work 1 standing dc, 2 dc, and 1 hdc around 1st ch; 1 sl st between next 2 dc; *around next ch, work 1 hdc, 2 dc, and 1 hdc; 1 sl st between next 2 dc*; rep * to * 4 more times, cut yarn, and end with 1 invisible sl st into the standing dc = 6 hdc-dc groups.

Rnd 3: With Yarn C, work 1 standing sc and 2 sc in the 1st dc of a group; *[1 hdc in next dc, dc2tog into next 2 hdc (crossing the gap between 2 groups), 1 hdc in same hdc as 2nd dc of dc2tog], 3 sc in next dc*; rep * to * 4 more times, rep within brackets once more, cut yarn, and end with 1 invisible sl st into the standing sc.

Rnd 4: With Yarn D, work 1 standing dc, ch 3, 1 dc into 2nd sc of a group of 3 sc; *[ch 1, skip 1 sc, 1 dc in next dc, ch 1, skip dc2tog, 1 dc in next dc], ch 1, skip 1 sc; in next sc, work 1 dc, ch 3, 1 dc*; rep * to * 4 more times, rep within brackets once more, cut yarn, and end with 1 invisible sl st into the standing dc.

Rnd 5: With Yarn D, work 1 standing tr and 8 tr around a loop of 3 ch; *[skip ch, 2 sc around next ch], skip ch, 9 tr around next loop of 3 ch*; rep * to * 4 more times, rep within brackets once more, cut yarn, and end with 1 invisible sl st into the standing tr.

Rnd 6: With Yarn E, work 1 standing tr into the 1st sc of a pair, ch 1, 1 tr in next sc, *[ch 1, skip 1 tr, 1 hdc in next tr, ch 1, skip 1 tr, 1 sc in each of next 3 tr, ch 1, skip 1 tr, 1 hdc in next tr], ch 1, skip 1 tr, 1 tr in next sc, ch 1, 1 tr in next sc*; rep * to * 4 more times, rep within brackets once more, cut yarn, and end with 1 invisible sl st into the standing tr.

Rnd 7: With Yarn E, work 1 standing dc into the hdc worked over the end of a fan of 9 tr, *[ch 3, work 2 front post tr tog around next 2 tr (= front post tr2tog), ch 3, 1 hdc in next dc, ch 3, 1 sc in each of next 2 sc], ch 3, skip 1 sc, 1 hdc in next dc*; rep * to * 4 more times, rep within brackets once more, ch 2, cut yarn, and end with 1 invisible sl st into the standing dc.

Rnd 8: With Yarn C, work 1 standing front post tr around a front post tr2tog; *[around next ch loop, work 1 tr and 4 dc; around next ch loop, work 1 hdc and 1 sc; 1 sc between next 2 sc; around next ch loop, work 1 sc and 1 hdc; around next ch loop, work 4 dc and 1 tr], work 1 front post tr around next front post tr2tog*; rep * to * 4 more times, work within brackets once more, cut yarn, and end with 1 invisible sl st into the standing tr.

Rnd 9: With Yarn B, work 1 standing front post tr around a front post tr; *[working in back loops only: 1 tr in next tr, 1 dc in each of next 2 dc, 2 dc in next dc; ch 1, skip 3 sts, 1 tr in next sc, ch 1, skip 3 sts; working in back loops only: 2 dc in next dc, 1 dc in each of next 2 dc, 1 tr in next tr]; 1 front post tr around next front post tr*; rep * to * 4 more times, rep within brackets once more, cut yarn, and end with 1 invisible sl st into the standing tr.

Weave in ends. Position work inside the inner circle of the embroidery hoop.

Rnd 10: With Yarn A, work 1 standing sc into a front post tr, capturing the inner circle of the embroidery hoop inside the st. *1 sc in next tr, worked around embroidery hoop; 1 sc in back loop only in each of next 4 dc, ch 2, 1 sc around embroidery hoop, ch 2, skip 1 ch and 1 tr, 1 sc in back loop only in ch and each of next 3 dc; 1 sc in dc and each of next 2 tr, worked around embroidery hoop*; rep * to * 5 more times, ending with 1 sc in last tr (instead of 2 tr) and around embroidery hoop. Cut yarn, and end with 1 invisible sl st into the standing sc.

Weave in ends. Secure the outer circle of the embroidery hoop around the inner circle, aligning the work relative to the hoop's screw as shown in the photo on page 18 before tightening the screw.

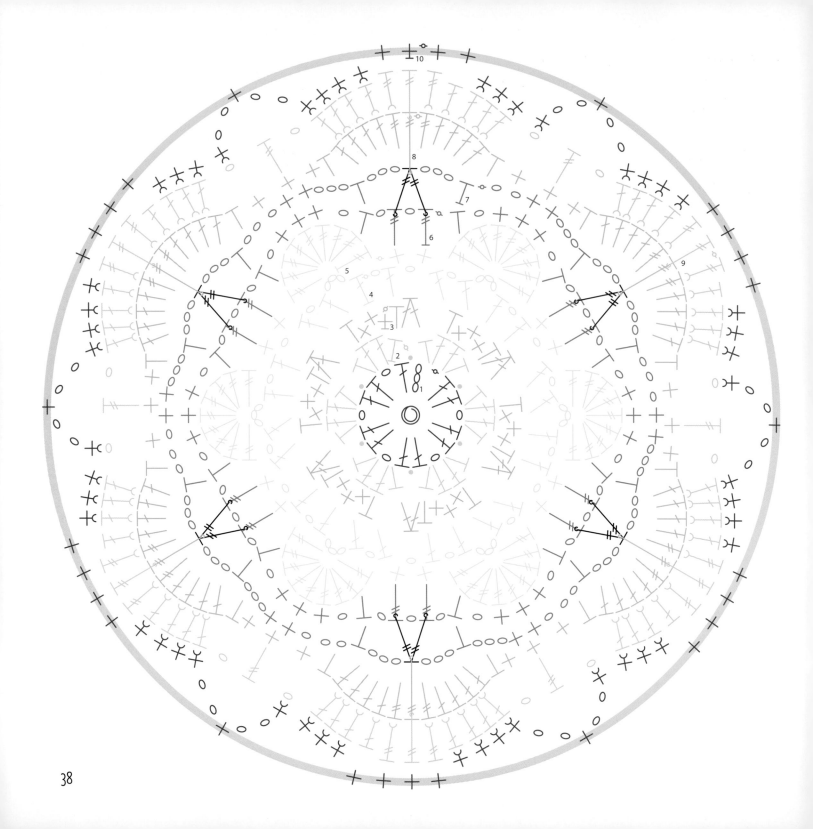

38

◎ magic ring

○ chain stitch

● slip stitch

-o- invisible slip stitch

+ single crochet

T half double crochet

Ŧ double crochet

Ŧ treble crochet

Ⱥ dc2tog

Ŧ front post treble crochet

 front post tr2tog

i standing stitch

人 stitch in back loop only

— Yarn A
— Yarn B
— Yarn C
— Yarn D
— Yarn E
— embroidery hoop

On Rnd 7 (Yarn E), the front post treble crochets are marked in black for clarity.

SMALL FLOWER TAMBOURINE

photos pages 18-19

MATERIALS	Diameter after blocking: 6½ in / 16.5 cm	Difficulty: simple
CYCA #3 (DK/light worsted) DMC Tapestry Wool Colbert (100% wool; 42 yd/38 m / 20 g), 20 g of each of the following: Blue-Green 7296 (A), sky blue (B), lemon-yellow (C), mauve (D) 1 embroidery hoop, 6½ in / 16.5 cm in diameter	Crochet hook, U.S. size 7 / 4.5 mm For hoop: sky blue paint and paintbrush For finishing: tapestry needle, pair of scissors, basin of water, blocking mat (or other surface), pins, drawing compass	

PATTERN STITCH

Front post treble crochet around a chain stitch two rounds below

Wrap the yarn around the hook twice. Insert the hook above a chain stitch two rounds below, from front to back, so it re-emerges beneath the chain. Wrap the yarn around the hook again and complete the treble crochet as usual.

Paint both parts of the embroidery hoop separately and let dry.

With Yarn A, make a magic ring.

Rnd 1: Work 6 sc into ring, ending with 1 sl st into the 1st sc. Tighten ring.

Rnd 2: Ch 1 (= 1 sc), 1 sc at the base of this sc, 2 sc in each additional sc around, and end with 1 sl st into the ch.

Rnd 3: Ch 1 (= 1 sc), 1 sc at the base of this sc, ch 1, *1 sc in each of next 2 sc, ch 1*; rep * to * 4 more times and end with 1 sl st into the 1st ch.

Rnd 4: Ch 3 (= 1 dc), 2 dc in 1st sc, ch 1, skip 1 ch, *1 dc in next sc, 2 dc in next sc, ch 1, skip 1 ch*; rep * to * 4 more times, cut yarn, and end with 1 invisible sl st into the 3rd ch.

Rnd 5: With Yarn B, work 1 standing sc into a dc not part of a pair of dc worked into the same st. *[Ch 1, skip 1 dc, 2 sc in next dc, 1 front post tr around next ch from Rnd 3], 1 sc in next dc*; rep * to * 4 more times, rep within brackets once more, and end with 1 sl st into the standing sc.

Rnd 6: Ch 4 (= 1 dc + 1 ch), skip 1 ch, 1 dc in each of next 2 sc, 2 dc in next tr, *1 dc in next sc, ch 1, skip 1 ch, 1 dc in each of next 2 sc, 2 dc in next tr*; rep * to * 4 more times, cut yarn, and end with 1 invisible sl st into the 3rd ch.

Rnd 7: With Yarn C, work 1 standing sc into the 1st dc of a group of 5 dc, 1 sc in each of next 4 dc, *[1 front post tr around next ch from Rnd 5, ch 1, 1 front post tr around that same ch again], 1 sc in each of next 5 dc*; rep * to * 4 more times, rep within brackets once more, and end with 1 sl st into the standing sc.

Rnd 8: Ch 1, 1 sc at the base of this ch, 1 sc in each of next 5 sc, skip 1 tr, 3 sc around next ch, *1 sc in next tr, 1 sc in each of next 5 sc, skip 1 tr, 3 sc around next ch*; rep * to * 4 more times, cut yarn, and end with 1 invisible sl st into the 1st sc.

Rnd 9: With Yarn D, work 1 standing dc in the 1st sc of a group of 3 sc situated between 2 tr from Rnd 7. 3 dc in same sc, 4 dc in each of next 2 sc, *[skip 2 sc, 1 sc in each of next 2 sc], skip 2 sc, 4 dc in each of next 3 sc*; rep * to * 4 more times, rep within brackets once more, cut yarn, and end with 1 invisible sl st into the standing dc.

Rnd 10: With Yarn A, work 1 standing sc in back loop only into one st. 1 sc in back loop only in all rem sts around, cut yarn, and end with 1 invisible sl st into the standing sc.

Rnd 11: With Yarn C, work 1 rnd of sl st between Rnds 9 and 10, cut yarn, and end with 1 invisible sl st into 1st sl st.

With Yarn D and tapestry needle, embroider a flower with six "lazy daisy" stitches at center of work (see photos on pages 18 and 19), passing the yarn under the treble crochet stitches worked with Yarn B on Round 5.

Key

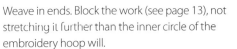

- ◎ magic ring
- ⬯ chain stitch
- ● slip stitch
- ⟳ invisible slip stitch
- + single crochet
- ‡ standing single crochet
- ⼊ single crochet in back loop only
- ┬ double crochet
- ⊥ standing double crochet
- ╪ front post treble crochet

— Yarn A
— Yarn B
— Yarn C
— Yarn D

Weave in ends. Block the work (see page 13), not stretching it further than the inner circle of the embroidery hoop will.

Attach the work to the inner circle of the embroidery hoop, using Yarn A to work 3 or 4 sc at the end of each "petal" and capturing the hoop inside the stitches. Weave in these ends also. Secure the outer circle of the embroidery hoop around the inner circle, aligning the work relative to the hoop's screw as shown in the photo on page 18 before tightening the screw.

Note

Even though the work will be stretched over the embroidery hoop, it's still important to block carefully.

RUDBECKIA

photos page 20

MATERIALS	Diameter after blocking: 5¾ in / 14.5 cm	Difficulty: intermediate
CYCA #0 (lace/fingering) DMC Pearl Cotton size 3 (100% cotton; 16 yd/15 m / 5 g), 5 g of each of the following: Yellow 307 (A), Pink 602 (B), Violet 550 (C), Green 911 (D)	Crochet hook, U.S. size B-1/C-2 / 2.5 mm For finishing: tapestry needle, pair of scissors, basin of water, blocking mat (or other surface), pins, drawing compass	

With Yarn A, make a magic ring.

Rnd 1: Ch 5 (= 1 tr + 1 ch), *1 tr into ring, ch 1*; rep * to * 10 more times, ending with 1 sl st into the 3rd ch instead of 1 ch = 24 sts. Tighten ring.

Rnd 2: Ch 6 (= 1 dc + 1 3-ch loop), skip 1 ch, *1 dc in next tr, ch 3, skip 1 ch*; rep * to * around, ending with 1 invisible sl st (you will need to cut yarn) in the 3rd ch instead of 1 ch = 12 dc and 12 ch loops.

Rnd 3: With Yarn B, dc4tog around a ch loop (work the first as a standing dc), *ch 4, skip 1 dc, dc4tog around next ch loop*; rep * to * 10 more times, ch 3, cut yarn, and end with 1 invisible sl st into the standing dc = 12 groups of dc4tog and 12 ch loops.

Rnd 4: With Yarn C, work 1 standing sc into a dc4tog, *5 sc around next ch loop, 1 sc into next dc4tog*; rep * to * 10 more times, work 5 sc around last ch loop, cut yarn, and end with 1 invisible sl st into the standing sc = 72 sc.

Rnd 5: Beg this rnd working into an sc situated vertically in line with an sc from Rnd 3 that's positioned right before a dc4tog. With Yarn D, work 1 standing sc in back loop only into this sc, *1 front post dc around next

dc4tog from Rnd 3, skip 1 sc, 1 sc in back loop only in each of next 5 sc*; rep * to * around, ending last rep with 1 sc in back loop only in each of next 4 sc instead of next 5, and then end rnd with 1 sl st into back loop only of the standing sc = 72 sts.

Rnd 6: Ch 1, sc in back loop only around, cut yarn, and end with 1 invisible sl st in back loop only into the 1st sc = 72 sc.

Rnd 7: Beg this rnd working into an sc situated vertically in line with a front post dc from Rnd 5. With Yarn A, work 1 standing sc in back loop only into this sc, *ch 7, skip 5 sc, 1 sc in back loop only in next sc*; rep * to * 10 more times, ch 7, cut yarn, and end with 1 sl st into the standing sc = 12 "petals" around.

Rnd 8: Ch 1; around each ch loop, work 3 sc, 2 hdc, 3 dc, 2 hdc, and 3 sc. Cut yarn and end with 1 invisible sl st into the 1st sc = 13 sts worked into each petal.

Rnd 9: Beg this rnd working into the dc in the center of a group of 3 dc from the prev rnd. With Yarn C, work 1 standing dc in back loop only and 2 dc in back loop only into this dc, *[2 dc in back loop only in next dc, 1 sc in back loop only in each of next 3 sts, 1 dtr in front loop only in the center sc of a

preceding group of 5 sc from Rnd 4, skip 1 sc, 1 sc in back loop only in each of next 2 sc, 1 treble dc in front loop only in the center sc of next group of 5 sc from Rnd 4, skip 1 sc, 1 sc in back loop only in each of next 3 sts, 2 dc in back loop only in next dc], 3 dc in back loop only in next dc*; rep * to * 10 more times, rep within brackets once more, cut yarn, and end with 1 invisible sl st in back loop only into the standing dc = 17 sts per petal.

Rnd 10: With Yarn B, work 1 standing sc in back loop only into an sc following a group of 7 dc, *[1 sc in back loop only in each of next 2 sc, skip 1 dtr, 1 dtr in front loop only in the same sc as in Rnd 9 (preceding group of 5 sc), skip 2 sc, 1 dtr in front loop only in the same sc as in Rnd 9 (next group of 5 sc), skip 1 dtr, 1 sc in back loop only in each of next 6 st, 3 hdc in back loop only in next dc], 1 sc in back loop only in each of next 4 sts*; rep * to * 10 more times, rep within brackets once more, 1 sc in back loop only in each of last 3 dc, cut yarn, and end with 1 invisible sl st in back loop only into the standing sc.

Rnd 11: With Yarn D, work 1 standing sc in back loop only into an sc situated at the outermost point of a petal. 1 sc in back loop only in each of next 7 sts, *[skip 1 dtr, 1 front post trtr around next front post dc from Rnd 5, skip 1 dtr], 1 sc in back loop only in each of next 5 sts*; rep * to * 10 more times, rep within brackets once more, 1 sc in back loop only in each of last 7 sts, cut yarn, and end with 1 invisible sl st in back loop only into the standing sc = 15 sc per petal and 12 trtr.

Weave in ends. Block the work (see page 13), pinning so as to stretch the petals to their fullest extent.

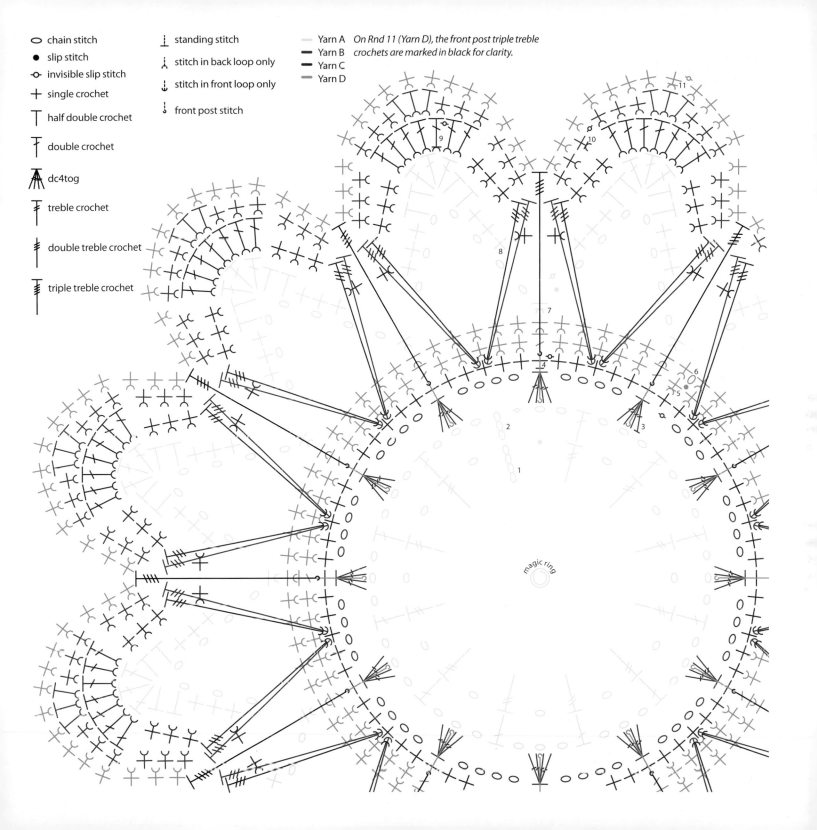

chain stitch
slip stitch
invisible slip stitch
single crochet
half double crochet
double crochet
dc4tog
treble crochet
double treble crochet
triple treble crochet

standing stitch
stitch in back loop only
stitch in front loop only
front post stitch

Yarn A
Yarn B
Yarn C
Yarn D

On Rnd 11 (Yarn D), the front post triple treble crochets are marked in black for clarity.

magic ring

POP!

photo page 21 - charts pages 46-47

MATERIALS	Diameter after blocking: 9¾ in / 25 cm	Difficulty: expert
CYCA #0 (lace/fingering) DMC Pearl Cotton size 3 (100% cotton; 16 yd/15 m / 5 g), 5 g each of Rose-Violet 718 (A), Yellow 307 (B), Violet 550 (E), Light Mauve 209 (F), Orange 947 (H); 10 g each of Green 959 (C), Dark Pink 601 (D), Dark Mauve 208 (G)		Crochet hook, U.S. size B-1/C-2 / 2.5 mm For finishing: tapestry needle, pair of scissors, basin of water, blocking mat (or other surface), pins, drawing compass; fabric stiffener and paintbrush (optional)

Note

Begin by crocheting eight small circles separately. These will be joined to the main work on Rnd 6. Rnds 10-14 are worked in overlay crochet (see page 11).

CIRCLES

With Yarn A, make a magic ring. Ch 2 (= 1 hdc), 11 hdc into ring, cut yarn, and end with 1 invisible sl st into the 2nd ch = 12 hdc. Tighten ring. Weave in ends. Make 7 more circles the same way.

MAIN WORK

With Yarn B, make a magic ring.

Rnd 1: Ch 3 (= 1 dc), 11 dc into ring, cut yarn, and end with 1 invisible sl st into the 3rd ch = 12 dc. Tighten ring.

Rnd 2: With Yarn C, work 1 standing sc and 1 sc into any dc. Work 2 sc into next dc around and end with 1 sl st into the standing sc = 24 sc.

Rnd 3: Ch 5 (= 1 dc + 1 ch loop), skip 1 sc, *1 dc in next sc, ch 2, skip 1 sc*; rep * to * 10 more times, and end with 1 invisible sl st (you will need to cut yarn) into the 3rd ch instead of ch 1 = 12 dc and 12 ch loops.

Rnd 4: With Yarn D, work 1 standing sc into any dc. *[2 tr in next sc of Rnd 2 that was skipped on Rnd 3], 1 sc in next dc*; rep * to * 10 more times, rep within brackets once more, cut yarn, and end with 1 invisible sl st into the standing sc = 36 sts.

Rnd 5: With Yarn C, work 1 standing sc into the 2nd tr of a pair of tr. *[1 front post dc around next dc of Rnd 3, skip 1 sc], 1 sc in each of next 2 tr*; rep * to * 10 more times, rep within brackets once more, 1 sc in last tr, cut yarn, and end with 1 invisible sl st into the standing sc.

Rnd 6: With Yarn B, 1 standing sc and 1 sc into one st, 2 sc in each of next 3 st, *[1 sc into both next st and one hdc of a circle, 1 sc in these same two sts, 2 sc in each of next 3 sts, 1 sc in next st, 1 sc into the same st and one hdc of a circle], 1 sc in each of next 4 sts*; rep * to * 2 more times, rep within brackets once more, cut yarn, and end with 1 invisible sl st into the standing sc = 72 sc.

Rnd 7: With Yarn E, work 1 standing dc between 2 sc situated at the center of one of the groups of 8 sc that separate two circles on Rnd 6. Ch 12. *1 dc in center of next 8 sc, ch 12*; rep * to * around and end with 1 sl st into the standing dc = 8 dc and 8 ch loops.

Rnd 8: Ch 1, *14 sc around next ch loop, 1 sl st into next dc*; rep * to * around, ending with 1 invisible sl st (you will need to cut yarn) into the ch instead of 1 regular sl st = 8 groups of 14 sc and 8 sl sts.

Rnd 9: With Yarn D, work 1 standing sc in back loop only into the 2nd sc of a group and 1 sc in back loop only into each of next 11 sc, *skip 3 sts, 1 sc in back loop only in each of next 2 sc*; rep * to * around, cut yarn, and end with 1 invisible sl st in back loop only into the standing sc = 8 groups of 12 sc.

Rnd 10: With Yarn F, work 1 standing sc in back loop only into the 4th sc of a group, *[2 sc in back loop only into next sc; working into a group from Rnd 8, 1 dc in front loop only into the 5th sc, skip 4 sc, 1 dc in front loop only into next sc; working into Rnd 9 again, skip 2 sc, 2 sc in back loop only in next sc, 1 sc in back loop only in next sc, 2 sc in back loop only in next sc; 1 incomplete sc in back loop only in next sc, skip 2 sc, 1 incomplete sc in back loop only in next sc, work these two sc tog = sc2tog with 2 sts skipped; 2 sc in back loop only in next sc], 1 sc in back loop only in next sc*; rep * to * 6 more times, rep within brackets once more, cut yarn, and end with 1 invisible sl st in back loop only into the standing sc = 8 groups of 12 sts and 8 individual sc.

Rnd 11: With Yarn G, work 1 standing sc in back loop only into the 2nd sc of a group, *[1 sc in back loop only in each of next 3 sc; working into Rnd 8, 1 tr in front loop only into 4th sc of group; working into Rnd 10, skip 1 dc, 2 sc in back loop only in next dc; working into Rnd 8, 1 tr in front loop only into the 11th sc of same group; working into Rnd 10, skip 1 sc, 2 sc in back loop only in each of next 2 sc, sc2tog with 2 sts skipped]; 1 sc in back loop only in next sc*. Rep * to * 6 more times, rep within brackets once more, and end with 1 invisible sl st in back loop only into the standing sc.

Rnd 12: With Yarn C, work 1 standing sc in back loop only and 1 sc in back loop only into the 3rd sc of a group, *[2 sc in back loop only in next sc; working into Rnd 8, 1 dtr in front loop only in the 3rd sc of a segment; working into Rnd 11, skip 1 tr, 1 sc in back loop only in next sc, 2 sc in back loop only in next sc; working into Rnd 8, 1 dtr in front loop only in the 12th sc of same group; working into Rnd 11, skip 1 tr, 2 sc in back loop only in each of next 3 sc, 1 sc in back loop only in next sc, skip 1 sc, 1 sc in back loop only in next sc], 2 sc in back loop only in each of next 2 sc*; rep * to * 6 more times, rep within brackets once more, 2 sc in back loop only in last sc, cut yarn, and end with 1 invisible sl st in back loop only into the standing sc = 8 groups of 19 sts.

Rnd 13: With Yarn B, work 1 standing sc in back loop only into the 3rd sc of a group, 1 sc in back loop only in each of next 4 sc, *[working into Rnd 8, 1 trtr in front loop only in the 2nd sc of a group; working into Rnd 12, skip 1 dtr, 1 sc in back loop only in each of next 3 sc; working into Rnd 8, 1 trtr in front loop only in the 13th sc of same group, working into Rnd 12, skip 1 dtr, 1 sc in back loop only in each of next 5 sc, sc2tog with 2 sts skipped], 1 sc in back loop

only in each of next 5 sc*; rep * to * 6 more times, rep within brackets once more, cut yarn, and end with 1 invisible sl st in back loop only into the standing sc = 8 groups of 15 sts and 8 individual sc.

Rnd 14: With Yarn H, work 1 standing sc in back loop only into the 2nd sc of a group, *[1 sc in back loop only in each of next 3 sc; working into Rnd 8, 1 quadtr in front loop only in the 1st sc of a group; working into Rnd 13, skip 1 trtr, 1 sc in back loop only in each of next 3 sc; working into Rnd 8, 1 quadtr in front loop only in the 14th sc of same group; working into Rnd 13, skip 1 trtr, 1 sc in back loop only in each of next 4 sc, sc2tog with 2 sts skipped], 1 sc in back loop only in next sc*; rep * to * 6 more times, rep within brackets once more, cut yarn, and end with 1 invisible sl st in back loop only into the standing sc = 8 groups of 13 sts and 8 individual sc.

Rnd 15: With Yarn E, work 1 standing dc in back loop only into any st; 1 dc in back loop only in each of next 6 sts, 2 dc in back loop only in next st, *1 dc in back loop only in each of next 7 sts, 2 dc in back loop only in next st*; rep * to * around, cut yarn, and end with 1 invisible sl st in back loop only into the standing dc = 126 dc.

Rnd 16: With Yarn C, work 1 standing sc into any dc, *ch 5, skip 4 dc, 1 sc in each of next 2 dc*; rep * to * around, ending with 1 sc in next dc and then 1 sl st into the standing sc = 21 ch loops and 21 pairs of sc.

Rnd 17: 1 sl st into sc and in each of next 3 ch, *ch 6, 2 sc around next ch loop*; rep * to * around until last ch loop, ch 6, and end with 1 sl st into the 3rd sl st.

Rnd 18: 1 sl st into each of first 5 sts, *ch 7, 2 sc around next ch loop*; rep * to * around until last ch loop, ch 7, cut yarn, and end with 1 invisible sl st into the 4th sl st.

Rnd 19: With Yarn F, work 1 standing sc in the 1st sc of a pair, *[1 sc in next sc, 7 sc around next ch loop, 1 sc in next sc], rep within brackets 5 more times, 1 sc in next sc, 8 sc around next ch loop, 1 sc in next sc*; rep * to * 2 more times, cut yarn, and end with 1 invisible sl st into the standing sc = 192 sc.

Rnd 20: With Yarn G, work 1 standing dc in back loop only into any sc, and then dc in back loops only around. Cut yarn and end with 1 invisible sl st in back loop only into the standing dc = 192 dc.

Rnd 21: Beg this rnd working into a dc situated along the central axis of one of the semicircles of Rnds 9-14. With Yarn D, work 1 standing sc in back loop only into this dc, 1 sc in back loop only in each of next 10 dc, *[1 picot (= 1 sl st, ch 3, 1 sl st) in next dc, 1 sc in back loop only in each of next 11 dc; working into Rnd 19, 1 tr in front loop only in the sc situated 5 sc previous; working into Rnd 20, 1 flower (= 1 sl st, ch 6, 1 sl st, ch 9, 1 sl st, ch 6, 1 sl st) in next dc; working into Rnd 19, count 9 sc after the previous tr and work 1 tr in front loop only in next sc]; working into Rnd 20, 1 sc in back loop only in each of next 11 dc*; rep * to * 6 more times, rep within brackets once more, cut yarn, and end with 1 invisible sl st in back loop only into the standing sc.

Weave in ends. Block the work; if you want to hang this mandala on your wall, it also might be a good idea to use some fabric stiffener (see page 13).

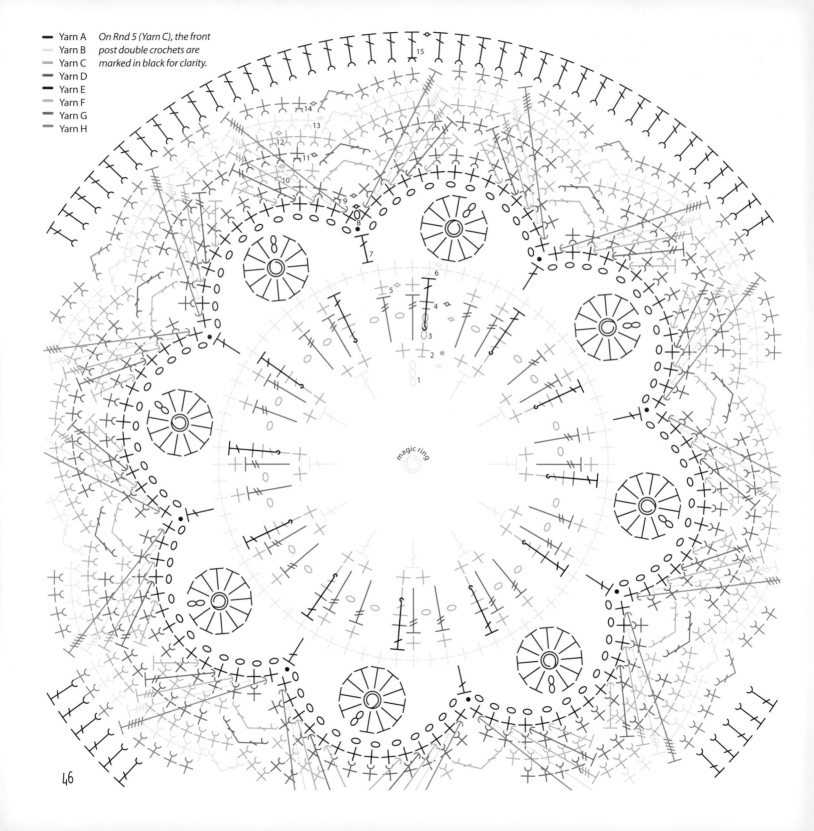

Yarn A
Yarn B
Yarn C
Yarn D
Yarn E
Yarn F
Yarn G
Yarn H

On Rnd 5 (Yarn C), the front post double crochets are marked in black for clarity.

magic ring

46

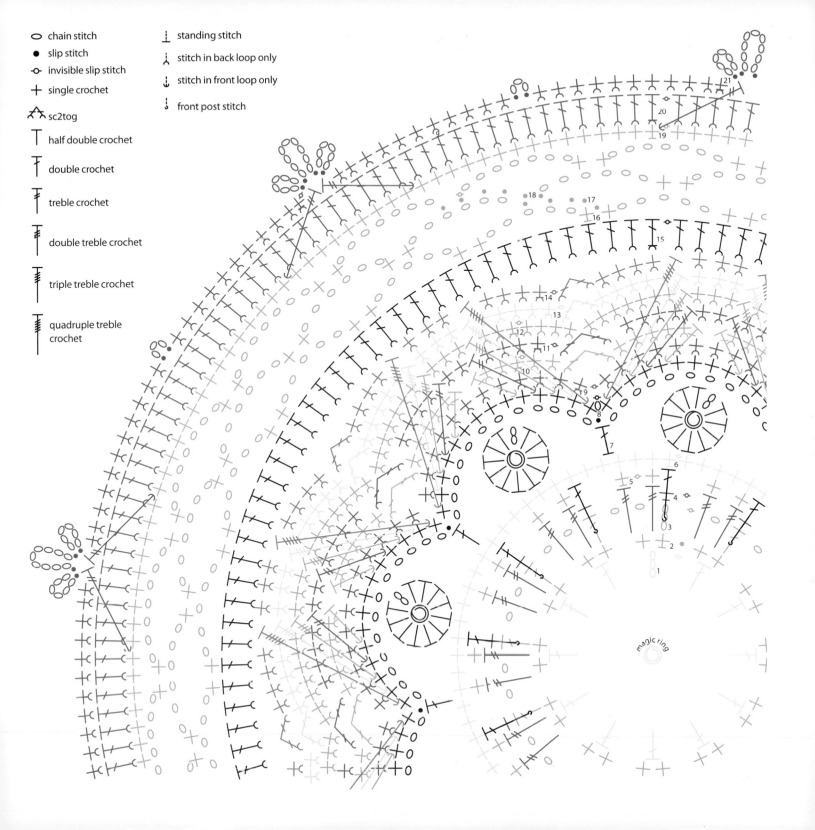

chain stitch
slip stitch
invisible slip stitch
single crochet
sc2tog
half double crochet
double crochet
treble crochet
double treble crochet
triple treble crochet
quadruple treble crochet
standing stitch
stitch in back loop only
stitch in front loop only
front post stitch

magic ring

DAHLIA

photos page 22

MATERIALS	Diameter after blocking: 9¾ in / 26 cm	Difficulty: expert
CYCA #2 (sport/baby) DMC Woolly Natural Knitting (100% merino wool; 136 yd/124 m / 50 g), 50 g each of the following: Violet 065 (A), Yellow 093 (B), Orange 103 (C) CYCA #3 (DK/light worsted) Patons Astra (100% acrylic; 161 yd/147 m / 50 g): 50 g of Hot Pink (D)	1 embroidery hoop, 10¼ in / 26 cm in diameter Crochet hook, U.S. size G-6 / 4 mm For finishing: tapestry needle, pair of scissors, yellow paint, and paintbrush	

Paint both parts of the embroidery hoop separately and let dry.

With Yarn A, make a magic ring.

Rnd 1: 8 sc into ring, cut yarn, and end with 1 invisible sl st in the 1st sc. Tighten ring.

Rnd 2: With Yarn B, work 1 standing sc and 1 sc into any sc; 2 sc into next sc around, cut yarn, and end with 1 invisible sl st into the standing sc = 16 sc.

Rnd 3: With Yarn A, work 1 standing sc into any sc, *2 sc in next sc, 1 sc in next sc*; rep * to * 6 more times, working 2 sc into last sc of rnd. Cut yarn and end with 1 invisible sl st into the standing sc = 24 sc.

Rnd 4: With Yarn D, work 1 standing dc into any sc, *[ch 3, 1 trtr in next sc], ch 3, 1 dc in next sc*; rep * to * 10 more times, rep within brackets once more, ch 2, cut yarn, and end with 1 invisible sl st into the standing dc = 12 "petals".

Rnd 5: With Yarn A, work 1 standing sc into a trtr, *ch 4, 1 sc in next trtr*; rep * to * 10 more times, ch 3, and end with 1 sl st into the standing sc = 12 ch loops.

Rnd 6: Ch 3 (= 1 dc), *[ch 4, 1 dc around next ch loop, ch 4, 1 dc around next ch loop just after sc, ch 4], 1 dc in next sc*; rep * to * 4 more times, rep within brackets once more, cut yarn, and end with 1 invisible sl st into the 3rd ch at beg = 18 ch loops.

Rnd 7: With Yarn C, work 1 standing sc into any dc; *[work 1 hdc, 1 dc, 1 tr, 1 dc, and 1 hdc around next ch loop]; 1 sc in next dc*; rep * to * 16 more times, rep within brackets once more, cut yarn, and end with 1 invisible sl st into the standing sc = 108 sts.

Rnd 8: Work all sts this rnd in back loops only. With Yarn B, work 1 standing tr into any sc, *[1 dc in next dc, 1 hdc in next dc, 1 sc in next tr, 1 hdc in next dc, 1 dc in next dc], 1 tr in next sc*; rep * to * 16 more times, rep within brackets once more, and end with 1 sl st into the standing tr.

Rnd 9: Ch 4 (= 1 dc + 1 ch), skip 1st tr, *1 dc in next st, ch 1, skip 1 st*; rep * to * around, ending with 1 invisible sl st (you will need to cut yarn) into the 3rd ch at beg instead of a ch.

Rnd 10: With Yarn A, work 1 standing sc into any dc, *[working into Rnd 8, 1 tr in front loop only in next st], 1 sc in next dc*; rep * to * until last dc, rep within brackets once more, cut yarn, and end with 1 invisible sl st into the standing sc.

Rnd 11: With Yarn D, work 1 standing dc into any tr, *ch 3, skip 1 sc, 1 dtr in next tr, ch 3, skip 1 sc, 1 dc in next tr*; rep * to * until last tr, ch 2, cut yarn, and end with 1 invisible sl st into the standing dc.

Rnd 12: With Yarn A, work 1 rnd of sl st between Rnds 7 and 8, cut yarn, and end with 1 invisible sl st into the 1st sl st.

Weave in ends. Secure work to inner circle of embroidery hoop with a long strand of Yarn D threaded onto a tapestry needle: Insert the needle into a dtr on Rnd 11, from back to front; wrap the yarn three times around the inner circle of the embroidery hoop; and then insert the needle into the next dtr on Rnd 11, from back to front. Continue around until you've worked through all dtrs on Rnd 11, and then slide the wrapped yarn around the inner circle until everything is evenly spaced. Weave in ends of the strand of Yarn D. Secure the outer circle of the embroidery hoop around the inner circle, aligning the work relative to the hoop's screw as shown in the photo on page 22 before tightening the screw.

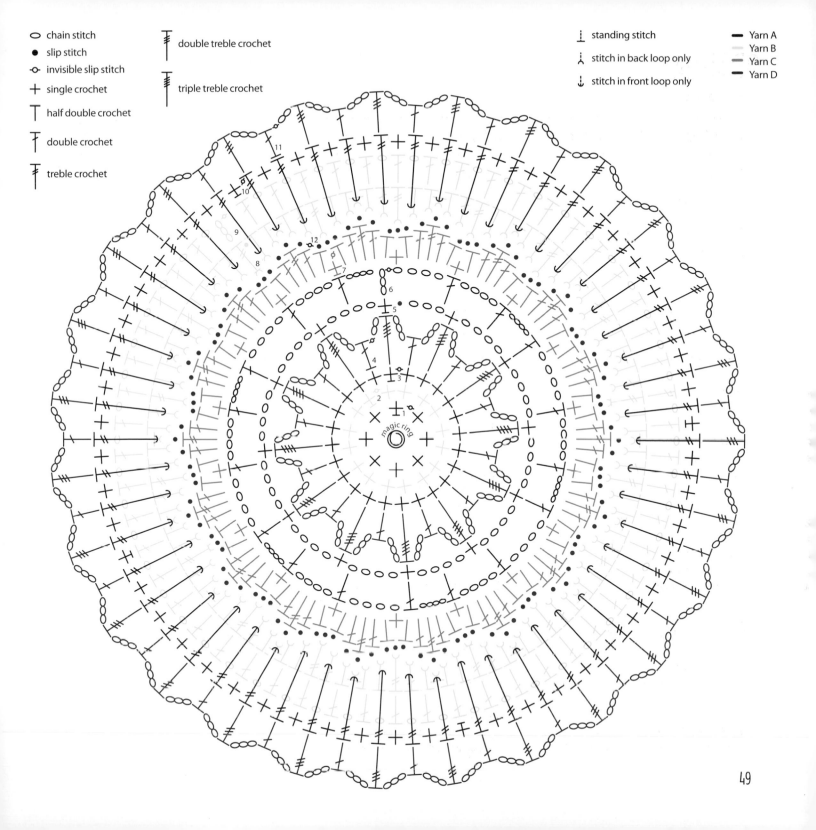

chain stitch
slip stitch
invisible slip stitch
single crochet
half double crochet
double crochet
treble crochet
double treble crochet
triple treble crochet
standing stitch
stitch in back loop only
stitch in front loop only
Yarn A
Yarn B
Yarn C
Yarn D

magic ring

49

COMPASS ROSE

photo page 23 - charts pages 52-53

MATERIALS	Diameter after blocking: 10¼ in / 26 cm	Difficulty: expert
CYCA #0 (lace/fingering) DMC Petra Crochet Cotton 5 (100% mercerized cotton, 437 yd/400 m / 100 g), 100 g of each of the following: Fuchsia 53805 (A), Pastel Pink 54461 (B), Black 5310 (C), Burgundy 5815 (D) CYCA #0 (lace/fingering) DMC Pearl Cotton size 5 (100% cotton; 27 yd/25 m / 5 g), 5 g of Mauve	451 (E) Crochet hook, U.S. size B-1 / 2 mm For finishing: tapestry needle, pair of scissors, basin of water, blocking mat (or other surface), pins, drawing compass	

PATTERN STITCH

4 "dodecuple" double crochets worked together (dodecuple dc4tog)

Wrap the yarn around the hook 12 times. Insert the hook into a stitch; *wrap the yarn around the hook once and pull through the stitch. [Wrap the yarn around the hook again and pull through the first 2 loops on the hook], rep within brackets 11 times (= 2 loops remaining on the hook)*. Rep * to * in each of next 3 stitches (= 5 loops on the hook). Wrap the yarn around the hook once and pull through all 5 loops.

COMPASS POINTS

With Yarn A, make a magic ring.

Rnd 1: 10 sc into ring, cut yarn, and end with 1 invisible sl st into the 1st sc. Tighten ring.

Rnd 2: With Yarn B, work 1 standing sc and 1 sc into any sc, *1 hdc and 1 tr in next sc, 1 hdc and 1 sc in next sc, 1 sc and 1 hdc in next sc, 1 tr and 1 hdc in next sc*, 2 sc in next sc; rep * to * once more, cut yarn, and end with 1 invisible sl st into the standing sc = 20 sts.

Rnd 3: With Yarn C, work 1 standing sc in the 1st sc of a pair. 1 sc in each of next 2 sts; *[2 sc, ch 3, 2 sc in next tr]; 1 sc in each of next 4 sts*; rep * to * 2 more times, rep within brackets once more, 1 sc in last hdc, cut yarn, and end with 1 invisible sl st intp the standing sc = 32 sc and 4 ch loops.

Rnd 4: With Yarn E, work 1 standing dc into an sc following a ch loop. 1 hdc in each of next 7 sc; *[work 1 dc, 1 tr, 1 dc around next ch loop]; 1 hdc in each of next 8 sc*; rep * to * 2 more times, rep within brackets once more, cut yarn, and end with 1 invisible sl st into the standing sc = 44 sts.

Rnd 5: With Yarn C, work 1 standing sc into any st; sc around, cut yarn, and end with 1 invisible sl st into the standing sc = 44 sc.

Make three more compass points the same way. Weave in ends and block all four compass points points (see page 13).

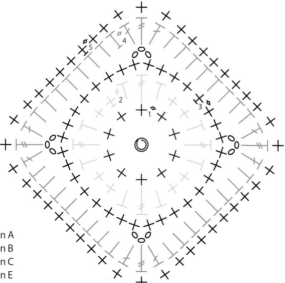

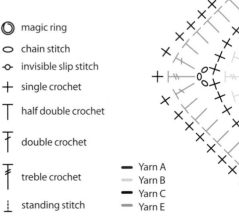 magic ring	
◠ chain stitch	
-o- invisible slip stitch	
+ single crochet	
T half double crochet	
⊤ double crochet	
⌅ treble crochet	
⊥ standing stitch	

— Yarn A
— Yarn B
— Yarn C
— Yarn E

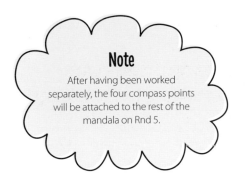

Note

After having been worked separately, the four compass points will be attached to the rest of the mandala on Rnd 5.

MAIN WORK

With Yarn C, make a magic ring.

Rnd 1: 8 sc into ring, cut yarn, and end with 1 invisible sl st into the 1st sc. Tighten ring.

Rnd 2: With Yarn E, work 1 standing dc and 1 hdc into any sc; 2 hdc in next sc around, cut yarn, and end with 1 invisible sl st into the standing dc = 16 hdc.

Rnd 3: With Yarn C, work 1 standing sc and 1 sc into any hdc; 2 sc in next hdc around, cut yarn, and end with 1 invisible sl st into the standing sc = 32 sc.

Rnd 4: Begin with Yarn A in any sc. *[Ch 15, skip 1 sc, dodecuple dc4tog into next 4 sc, ch 15, skip 1 sc], 1 sl st into each of next 2 sc*; rep * to * 2 more times, rep within brackets once more, 1 sl st into last sc, cut yarn, and end with 1 invisible sl st into 1st ch = 4 "petals" and 4 pairs of sl sts.

Weave in ends.

Rnd 5: With Yarn D, work 1 sl st into the 2nd sl st of a pair. Ch 12, 1 sc in each of 11 sc of lower left side of a compass point, *[ch 19, 1 sc in the point of the next "petal", ch 6, turn; skip 1 ch, 1 sl st into next ch, 1 sc in next ch, 1 hdc in next ch, 1 dc in next ch, 1 tr in next ch, 1 dtr in next sc, 1 tr in next ch, 1 dc in next ch, 1 hdc in next ch, 1 sc in next ch, 1 sl st in next ch, turn; skip 1 sl st, 1 sl st into each of next 4 st, skip 1 dtr, 1 sl st into each of next 4 st, ch 15], 1 sc in each of 11 sc of lower right side of next compass point, ch 12, 1 sl st into each of next 2 sl st, 1 sl st into each of 12 ch, 1 sc in each of 11 sc of lower left side of same compass point*; rep * to * 2 more times, rep within brackets once more, 1 sc in each of 11 sc of lower right side of 1st compass point, 1 sl st into each of first 12 ch. Cut yarn and end with 1 invisible sl st into last sl st of Rnd 4.

Rnd 6: Beg rnd working into upper right side of a compass point. With Yarn A, *counting from bottom up, skip 5 sc in Yarn C; work 1 sl st into next sc, 1 sc in each of next 2 sc, 1 hdc in next sc, 2 dc in next sc; work 1 tr, 1 dtr, 1 trtr, 1 dtr, 1 tr into next sc; 2 dc in next sc, 1 hdc in next sc, 1 sc in each of next 2 sc, 1 sl st into next sc, ch 17, 1 sc in last free ch of Rnd 5, 1 sc in each of next 10 sl sts, 1 sc in next free ch, ch 17*; rep * to * 3 more times, cut yarn, and end with 1 invisible sl st into the 1st sl st.

Rnd 7: With Yarn C, work 1 standing sc in back loop only in the 1st sc of a group of 15 sts situated at the top of a compass point. *[1 sc in back loop only in each of next 5 st, 2 sc in back loop only in next dtr, 3 sc in back loop only in next trtr, 2 sc in back loop only in next dtr, 1 sc in back loop only in each of next 6 st, 1 front post quadtr around an sc situated vertically in line with Rnd 1 of compass point, 35 sc or more around next ch loop (work as many as needed to hide Yarn A of ch loop completely), 1 sc in next sc, skip 4 sc, 2 dtr and 2 tr in next sc, ch 16, 1 sl st into the 2nd ch, ch 1, 2 tr and 2 dtr in next sc, skip 4 sc, 1 sc in next sc, 35 or more around next ch loop (work as many as needed to hide Yarn A of ch loop completely), 1 front post quadtr around an sc situated vertically in line with Rnd 1 of compass point], 1 sc in back loop only in next sc*; rep * to * 2 more times, rep within brackets once more, cut yarn, and end with 1 invisible sl st into the standing sc.

Weave in ends. Block the work.

Bonus idea

You can work this entire pattern in DMC Pearl Cotton size 5, if you want!

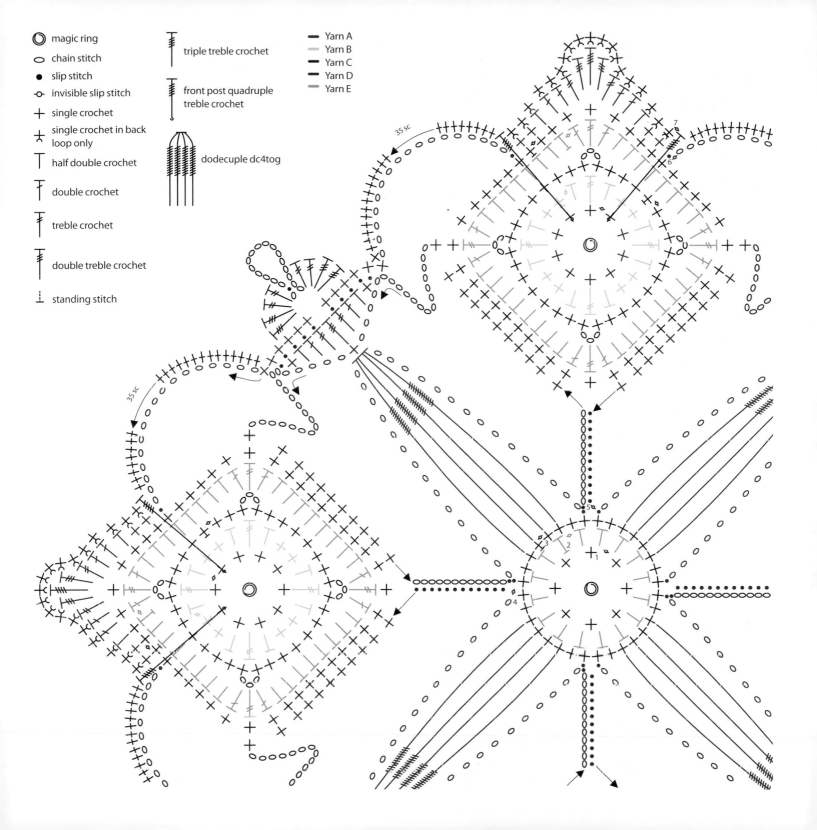

magic ring

chain stitch

slip stitch

invisible slip stitch

single crochet

single crochet in back
loop only

half double crochet

double crochet

treble crochet

double treble crochet

standing stitch

triple treble crochet

front post quadruple
treble crochet

dodecuple dc4tog

Yarn A
Yarn B
Yarn C
Yarn D
Yarn E

35 sc

35 sc

NORTHERN LIGHTS

photos page 24

photos page 24

MATERIALS	Diameter: 9¾ in / 25 cm	Difficulty: simple
CYCA #2 (sport/baby) DMC Woolly Natural Knitting (100% merino wool; 136 yd/124 m / 50 g), 50 g of each of the following: Red 051 (A), Burgundy 053 (B), Denim 072 (C), Glacier Blue 073 (D) 1 embroidery hoop, 9¾ in / 25 cm in diameter 1 flower-shaped button	1 rhinestone, 2 mm in diameter Sewing thread: colors matching Yarn D, colors matching the button Glue (to paste the rhinestone) Crochet hook, U.S. size G-6 / 4 mm For finishing: tapestry needle, sewing needle, pair of scissors	

With Yarn A, make a magic ring.

Rnd 1: Ch 4 (= 1 dc + ch 1), *1 dc into ring, ch 1*; rep * to * 5 more times, 1 sl st into the 3rd ch at beg = 14 sts. Tighten ring.

Rnd 2: Ch 4 (= 1 dc + ch 1), *1 dc around next ch, ch 1, 1 dc in next dc, ch 1*; rep * to * 5 more times, 1 dc around last ch, ch 1, 1 sl st into the 3rd ch at beg = 28 sts.

Rnd 3: *Ch 4, skip 3 sts, 1 sl st into next dc*; rep * to * 6 more times, working last sl st into the 1st ch = 7 ch loops and 7 sl st.

Rnd 4: *6 dc around next ch loop, 1 sl st into next sl st*; rep * to * 6 more times, working invisible sl st instead of last sl st (you will need to cut yarn) = 49 sts.

Rnd 5: With Yarn B, work 1 standing dtr into any sl st, *[ch 3, skip 2 dc, 1 sc in each of next 2 dc], ch 3, skip 2 dc, 1 dtr in next sl st*; rep * to * 5 more times, rep within brackets once more, ch 2, and end with 1 sl st into the standing dtr = 21 sts and 14 ch loops.

Rnd 6: Ch 3 (= 1 dc), 3 dc and 1 hdc around any ch loop, *[1 sc in each of next 2 sc, 1 hdc and 4 dc around next ch loop, 1 picot (= ch 3, 1 sl st into 1st ch)], skip 1 dtr, 4 dc and 1 hdc around next ch loop*; rep * to * 5 more times, rep within brackets once more, cut yarn, and end with 1 invisible sl st in the 3rd ch = 84 sts and 7 picots.

Rnd 7: With Yarn C, work 1 standing sc into any picot, *[ch 5, skip 6 sts, 1 dtr in next sc], ch 5, skip 5 sts, 1 sc in next picot*; rep * to * 5 more times, rep within brackets once more, ch 4, 1 sl st into the standing sc = 14 sts and 14 ch loops.

Rnd 8: Ch 3, *7 dc around next ch loop, 1 front post dc around next dtr, 7 dc around next ch loop, 1 front post dc around next sc*; rep * to * 6 more times (work last front post dc around the 3 ch at beg), cut yarn, and end with 1 invisible sl st in the 3rd ch = 112 sts.

Rnd 9: With Yarn D, work 1 standing dc into any dc; 1 dc in each dc and 1 front post dc around each front post dc around, cut yarn, and end with 1 invisible sl st in the standing dc.

Rnd 10: With Yarn A, work as for Rnd 9.

Rnd 11: With Yarn B, work as for Rnd 9.

Rnd 12: With Yarn D, work 1 standing dc and 1 dc into a dc preceding a front post dc. *1 front post dc around next front post dc, 1 dc in each of next 6 dc, 2 dc in next dc*; rep * to * 12 more times, 1 dc in each dc rem, cut yarn, and end with 1 invisible sl st in the standing dc = 126 sts.

Rnd 13: With Yarn C, work as for Rnd 9.

Rnd 14: With Yarn B, work as for Rnd 9.

Rnd 15: With Yarn D, work 1 standing dc and 1 dc into a dc following a front post dc. *1 dc in each of next 7 dc, 1 front post dc around next front post dc, 2 dc in next dc*; rep * to * 12 more times, 1 dc in each dc rem, cut yarn, and end with 1 invisible sl st in the standing dc = 140 sts.

Weave in ends. Thread Yarn D onto tapestry needle, wrap 5 times around every other dc on Rnd 2. Weave in ends of Yarn D.

With double strand of sewing thread that matches Yarn D, secure the work to the inner circle of the embroidery hoop: Insert the needle in the top of each dc of Rnd 15, then in the base of the same dc after passing thread around inner circle of embroidery hoop. Secure the outer circle of the embroidery hoop around the inner circle, aligning the work relative to the hoop's screw as shown in the photo on page 24 before tightening the screw. Glue the rhinestone in the center of the flower-shaped button, let dry, and then with sewing thread that matches button, secure button at center of work.

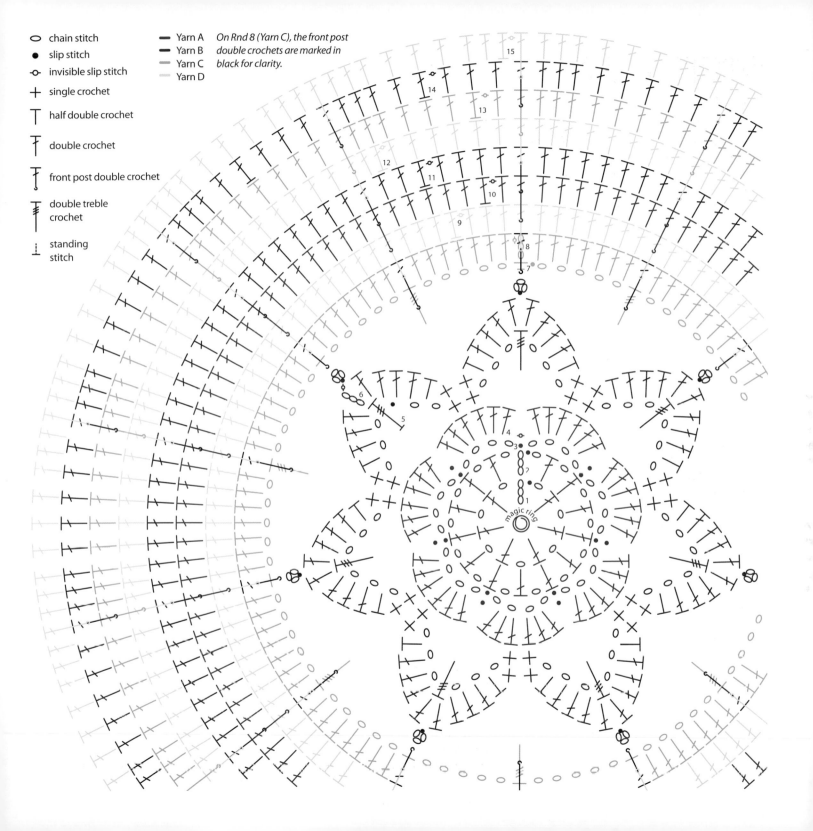

chain stitch
slip stitch
invisible slip stitch
single crochet
half double crochet
double crochet
front post double crochet
double treble crochet
standing stitch

Yarn A
Yarn B
Yarn C
Yarn D

On Rnd 8 (Yarn C), the front post double crochets are marked in black for clarity.

SEVENTIES

photo page 25 - charts pages 58-59

MATERIALS	Diameter after blocking: 15 in / 38 cm	Difficulty: intermediate
CYCA #2 (sport/baby) DMC Woolly Natural Knitting (100% merino wool; 136 yd/124 m / 50 g), 50 g of each of the following: Turquoise 074 (A), Violet 065 (B), Yellow 093 (C), Orange 103 (D) Crochet hook, U.S. size G-6 / 4 mm	For finishing: tapestry needle, pair of scissors, basin of water, blocking mat (or other surface), pins, drawing compass; fabric stiffener and brush (optional)	

With Yarn A, make a magic ring.

Rnd 1: Ch 3 (= 1 dc), 9 dc into ring, 1 sl st in the 3rd ch = 10 dc. Tighten ring.

Rnd 2: Ch 3 (= 1 dc), 1 dc into the base of these ch, 2 dc in each dc around, cut yarn, and end with 1 invisible sl st in the 3rd ch = 20 dc.

Rnd 3: With Yarn B, work 1 standing sc in the 2nd dc of a pair, *[1 sc in next dc, 1 front post dc around next dc of Rnd 1], 1 sc in next dc*; rep * to * 8 more times, rep within brackets once more, cut yarn, and end with 1 invisible sl st in the standing sc = 30 sts.

Rnd 4: With Yarn C, dc3tog (working 1st dc as standing dc) between 2 sc, ch 3, skip 1 front post dc, *dc3tog between next 2 sc, ch 3, skip 1 front post dc*; rep * to * 8 more times, working 1 invisible sl st (you will need to cut yarn) instead of ch 1 in 1st group of dc3tog = 10 groups of dc3tog and 10 ch loops.

Rnd 5: With Yarn B, work 1 standing sc and 1 sc around a ch loop, *[skip 1 group of dc3tog, 2 sc around next ch loop, 1 front post dc around front post dc of Rnd 3], 2 sc around same ch loop*; rep * to * 8 more times, rep within brackets once more, cut yarn, and end with 1 invisible sl st in the standing sc = 50 sts.

Rnd 6 (double rnd): With Yarn A, work 1 standing sc into 2nd sc after a front post dc, *[ch 10, skip 4 sts, 1 sc in next st], rep within brackets 8 more times, ch 9, cut yarn, and end with 1 invisible sl st in the standing sc*. With Yarn C, work 1 standing sc into front post dc, rep * to * once more = 20 sc and 20 ch loops.

Rnd 7: With Yarn D, work 1 standing dc and 2 dc into an sc worked with Yarn A, catching the ch loop worked in Yarn C with these sts; ch 2, 1 sc around next ch loop in Yarn A, ch 2, *3 dc in next sc in Yarn A, catching the ch loop worked in Yarn C; ch 2, 1 sc around next ch loop in Yarn A, ch 2*; rep * to * around, working 1 invisible sl st (you will need to cut yarn) instead of ch 1 in the standing dc = 80 sts.

Rnd 8: With Yarn D, work 1 standing dc into any st; dc around, cut yarn, and end with 1 invisible sl st in the standing dc = 80 dc.

Rnd 9: With Yarn C, work 1 standing sc into any dc, *ch 5, skip 4 dc, 1 sc in next dc*; rep * to * 14 more times, ch 4, cut yarn, and end with 1 invisible sl st in the standing sc = 16 sc and 16 ch loops.

Rnd 10: With Yarn B, dc7tog (working 1st dc as standing dc) around a ch loop, ch 3, 1 front post dc around next sc, ch 3, *dc7tog around next ch loop, ch 3, 1 front post dc in next sc, ch 3*; rep * to * around, working 1 invisible sl st (you will need to cut yarn) instead of ch 1 in the 1st dc7tog = 32 sts and 32 ch loops.

Rnd 11: With Yarn A, work 1 standing dc and 2 dc around a ch loop preceding a dc7tog, 1 front post dc around dc7tog, 3 dc around next ch loop, ch 1, skip 1 front post dc, *3 dc around next ch loop, 1 front post dc around next dc7tog, 3 dc around next ch loop, ch 1, skip 1 front post dc*; rep * to * around, working 1 invisible sl st (you will need to cut yarn) instead of ch 1 in the standing dc = 128 sts.

Rnd 12: With Yarn B, work 1 standing sc into any dc preceding a ch, *[1 front post dc around next front post dc of Rnd 10, 1 sc in next dc, ch 1, skip 1 dc, 1 sc in each of next 3 dc], ch 1, skip 1 dc, 1 sc in next dc*; rep * to * 14 more times, rep within brackets once more, cut yarn, and end with 1 invisible sl st in the standing sc.

Rnd 13: With Yarn C, dc3tog (working 1st dc as standing dc) into a ch, *ch 3, skip 3 sts, dc3tog in next ch*; rep * to * around until 3 sts rem, ch 2, cut yarn, and end with 1 invisible sl st into 1st dc3tog = 32 dc3tog and 32 ch loops.

Rnd 14: With Yarn B, work 1 standing sc and 2 sc around a ch loop situated vertically in line with a front post dc of Rnd 12, *1 front post tr around next front post dc of Rnd 12, 3 sc around same ch loop, skip 1 dc3tog, 3 sc around next ch loop], skip 1 dc2tog, 3 sc around next ch loop*; rep * to * around, ending last rep at closing bracket. Cut yarn and end with 1 invisible sl st in the standing sc = 160 sts.

Rnd 15 (double rnd): With Yarn A, work 1 standing sc in the 2nd sc after a front post dc, *[ch 10, skip 4 sts, 1 sc in next st], rep within brackets around until 4 sts rem, ch 9, cut yarn, and end with 1 invisible sl st in the standing sc*. With Yarn C, work 1 standing sc into a front post dc, rep * to * once more = 64 sc and 64 ch loops.

Rnd 16: With Yarn D, work 1 standing dc and 2 dc into an sc in Yarn A, catching the ch loop worked in Yarn C with these sts; ch 1, 1 sc around next ch loop in Yarn A, ch 1, *3 dc in next sc in Yarn A, catching the ch loop worked in Yarn C; ch 1, 1 sc around next ch loop in Yarn A, ch 1*; rep * to * around, working 1 invisible sl st (you will need to cut yarn) instead of ch 1 in the standing dc = 192 sts.

Rnd 17: With Yarn D, work 1 standing dc into any st; dc around, cut yarn, and end with 1 invisible sl st in the standing dc = 192 dc.

Rnd 18: With Yarn C, work 1 standing sc into any dc, *ch 7, skip 5 dc, 1 sc in next dc*; rep * to * around until 5 dc rem, ch 6, cut yarn, and end with 1 invisible sl st in the standing sc = 32 sc and 32 ch loops.

Rnd 19: With Yarn B, work 1 standing front post dc around any sc, *[ch 3, dc8tog around next ch loop], ch 3, 1 front post dc around next sc*; rep * to * around until 1 sc rem, rep within brackets once more, ch 2, cut yarn, and end with 1 invisible sl st in the standing front post dc = 64 sts and 64 ch loops.

Rnd 20: With Yarn A, work 1 standing dc into a front post dc, *[3 dc around next ch loop, 1 front post dc around next dc8tog, 3 dc around next ch loop], 1 dc in next front post dc*; rep * to * around until 1 front post dc rem, rep within brackets once more, and end with 1 sl st into the standing dc = 256 sts.

Rnd 21: Ch 1 (= 1 sc), *[1 hdc in next dc, 1 dc in next dc, 1 tr in each of next 2 dc, 1 dc in next dc, 1 hdc in next dc], 1 sc in each of next 2 dc*; rep * to * around until 7 dc rem, rep within brackets once more, 1 sc in last dc, cut yarn, and end with 1 invisible sl st in the 1st ch.

Rnd 22: With Yarn C, work 1 standing sc in back loop only between 2 sc, *[1 sc in back loop only in each of next 2 sts, 2 sc in back loop only in each of next 2 tr, 1 sc in back loop only in each of next 2 sts], 1 sc in back loop only between next 2 sc*; rep * to * around until 7 sts rem, rep within brackets once more, cut yarn, and end with 1 invisible sl st in back loop only in the standing sc = 224 sc.

Rnd 23: With Yarn C, work 1 rnd of ch around the stitch "posts" between Rnds 20 and 21, cut yarn, and end with 1 invisible sl st in the 1st ch (see photo on page 25).

Weave in ends. Block the work; if you want to hang this mandala on your wall, it also might be a good idea to use some fabric stiffener (see page 13).

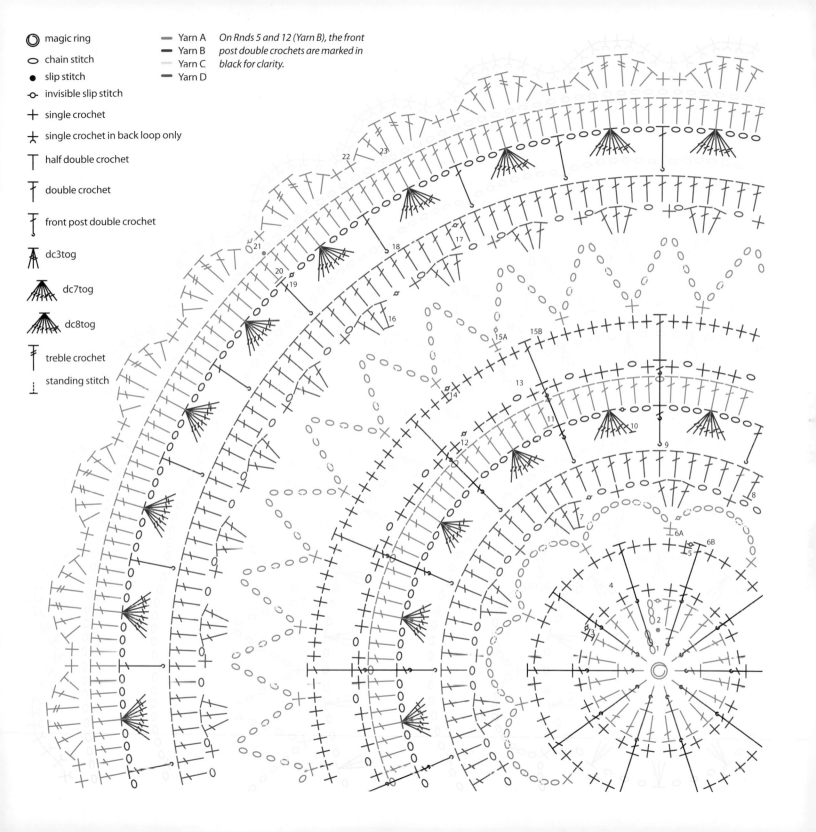

magic ring

chain stitch

slip stitch

invisible slip stitch

single crochet

single crochet in back loop only

half double crochet

double crochet

front post double crochet

dc3tog

dc7tog

dc8tog

treble crochet

standing stitch

Yarn A
Yarn B
Yarn C
Yarn D

On Rnds 5 and 12 (Yarn B), the front post double crochets are marked in black for clarity.

MANDALA PROJECTS

instructions for Millefiori Earrings on page 70

instructions for Sun Pendant on pages 72-73

instructions for Nigella Earrings on page 71

instructions for Mini-Mandala Bunting on pages 74-75

instructions for Coasters on pages 84-85

instructions for Dharma Bag on pages 87-89

instructions for Indian Garden Cushion pages 90-93

MILLEFIORI EARRINGS

photo page 61

MATERIALS	Diameter: 1½ in / 4 cm	Difficulty: simple
5 m of synthetic cord 1 mm in diameter, multicolored neon	6 small brass rings (or other metal that will not irritate your skin)	
2 small enameled triangles with pierced corners	Crochet hook, U.S. size B-1/C-2 / 2.5 mm	
2 small round brass charms (or other metal that will not irritate your skin)	Tapestry needle, pair of scissors, needlenose pliers for jewelry work	
1 pair of brass earring hooks (or other metal that will not irritate your skin)		

With the yarn, make a magic ring.

Rnd 1: Ch 3 (= 1 dc), 15 dc into ring, 1 sl st in the 3rd ch = 16 dc. Tighten ring.

Rnd 2: Ch 5 (= 1 sc + 1 ch loop), skip 1 dc, 1 sc in next dc, *ch 4, skip 1 dc, 1 sc in next dc*; rep * to * 5 more times, ch 4, cut yarn, and end with 1 invisible sl st in the 1st ch = 8 sc and 8 ch loops.

Work a second mini-mandala the same way. Weave in ends. Attach an earring hook to an sc at the top of each mini-mandala; using the 6 rings, attach the round brass charms to the corners of the enameled triangles (as shown in the photo on page 61), and then attach the triangles to the bottoms of the mini-mandalas.

Tip

You can change the number of double crochets if you use a cord of a different thickness—the only essential thing is that the total number of dc be even.

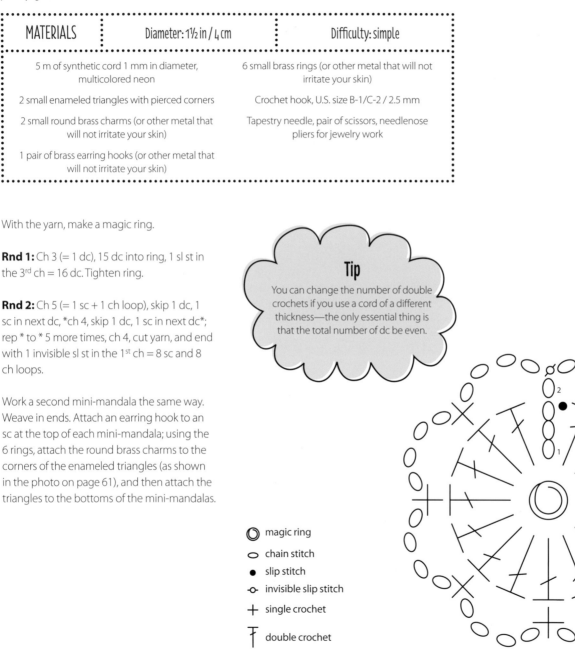

⊙ magic ring

○ chain stitch

● slip stitch

↻ invisible slip stitch

+ single crochet

Ŧ double crochet

NIGELLA EARRINGS

photo page 63

MATERIALS	Diameter: 1¼ in / 3 cm	Difficulty: intermediate
CYCA #0 (lace/fingering) DMC Cebelia Cotton size 30 (100% mercerized cotton; 567 yd/518 m / 50 g), a small amount of Black 310	2 clear rhinestones, ⅛ in / 4 mm in diameter	
	2 earring hoops, 1¼ in / 3 cm in diameter	
12 black multifaceted beads, ⅛ in / 4 mm in diameter	1 pair of earring hooks	
	Glue (to paste rhinestones)	
6 metal teardrop-shaped sequins	Crochet hook, U.S. steel size 10 / .75 mm	
(4 small and 2 large)	For finishing: fine embroidery needle, pair of scissors, needlenose pliers for jewelry work	
2 black oval rhinestones, ¼ in / 8 mm long		

PATTERN STITCH
Chain stitch with bead (ch w bead)
String a bead onto the yarn and slide it up next to the hook. Wrap the yarn around the hook and pull it through the working loop, as for any other chain stitch; then pull to tighten yarn and secure bead in place.

Open a hoop, slide 3 teardrop sequins onto it (1 large sequin with a smaller sequin on either side), then close the hoop again. String 5 beads onto the yarn.

With the yarn, make a magic ring.

Rnd 1: 5 sc into ring, 1 sl st into the 1st sc. Tighten ring.

Rnd 2: Ch 3 (= 1 dc), ch 1, 1 ch w bead, ch 1, *1 dc in next sc, ch 1, 1 ch w bead, ch 1*; rep * to * 3 more times and end with 1 sl st into the 3rd ch at beg.

Rnd 3: *Ch 8, 1 front post sc around next dc*; rep * to * around and end with 1 sl st into the 1st ch = 5 sc and 5 ch loops.

Rnd 4: Ch 1, *8 sc around next ch loop, 1 sl st around hoop, move yarn to front of work, 8 sc around same ch loop*; rep * to * for each ch loop around (work 1st sl st through the closure at the top of the hoop; make sure the sequins end up between the 3rd and 4th sl sts), cut yarn,

and end with 1 invisible sl st in the 1st sc.

Make a second earring the same way.

Weave in ends. Glue the round rhinestones in the centers of the mandalas and the oval rhinestones at the tops (see photo on page 63), and then let dry. Attach hoops to earring hooks.

- ⊚ magic ring
- ⬭ chain stitch
- ⬮ chain stitch with bead
- ● slip stitch
- ⊶ invisible slip stitch
- + single crochet
- ⊤ front post single crochet
- ⊤ double crochet
- ━ earring hoop

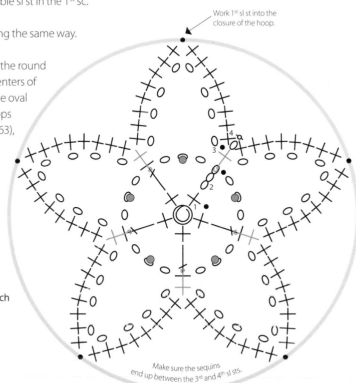

Work 1st sl st into the closure of the hoop.

Make sure the sequins end up between the 3rd and 4th sl sts.

SUN PENDANT

photo page 62

MATERIALS	Diameter after blocking: 2¼ in / 6 cm	Difficulty: intermediate
CYCA #0 (lace/fingering) DMC Cebelia Cotton size 30 (100% mercerized cotton; 567 yd/518 m / 50 g), small amounts of each of the following colors: Black 310 (A), Green 959 (B), Peach 754 (C) 1 black necklace cord with clasp 1 small metal ring		Crochet hook, U.S. steel size 10 / .75 mm Stitch marker For finishing: tapestry needle, pair of scissors, needlenose pliers for jewelry work, bowl of water, blocking mat (or other surface), pins, drawing compass

Note

This pattern is worked in tapestry crochet: carry unused yarn(s) along on wrong side and swap in as necessary for color changes (see page 11). Tapestry crochet should be done tightly!

With Yarn A, make a magic ring.

Rnd 1: Work 8 sc into ring. Tighten ring.

This design is worked in a spiral: Place stitch marker at beginning of Rnd 2 and move up to beginning of each subsequent rnd.

Rnd 2: 2 sc in each sc around = 16 sc.

Rnd 3: *1 sc in next sc, 2 sc in next sc*; rep * to * 7 more times = 24 sc.

Rnd 4: *1 sc in each of next 2 sc, 2 sc in next sc*; rep * to * 7 more times = 32 sc.

Rnd 5: *1 sc in each of next 3 sc, 2 sc in next sc*; rep * to * 7 more times = 40 sc.

Rnd 6: Move Yarn B to back to carry until needed. Work *1 sc in Yarn A in each of next 4 sc, 1 sc in Yarn A and 1 sc in Yarn B in next sc*; rep * to * 7 more times (with last yarnover in Yarn A) = 48 sc.

Rnd 7: *1 sc in Yarn A in each of next 4 sc, 2 sc in Yarn B in next sc, 1 sc in Yarn B in next sc*; rep * to * 7 more times (with last yarnover in Yarn A) = 56 sc.

Rnd 8: *1 sc in Yarn A in each of next 3 sc, 1 sc in Yarn B in each of next 3 sc, 2 sc in Yarn B in next sc*; rep * to * 7 more times (with last yarnover in Yarn A) = 64 sc.

Rnd 9: *1 sc in Yarn A in each of next 2 sc, 1 sc in Yarn B in each of next 5 sc, 2 sc in Yarn B in next sc*; rep * to * 7 more times (with last yarnover in Yarn A) = 72 sc.

Rnd 10: Move Yarn C to back to carry until needed. Work *1 sc in Yarn A in next sc, 1 sc in Yarn B in each of next 3 sc, 1 sc in Yarn B and 1 sc in Yarn C in next sc, 1 sc in Yarn B in each of next 4 sc*; rep * to * 7 more times = 80 sc.

Rnd 11: Yarn A will not be used again before cutting, but continue to carry along back of work. Work *1 sc in Yarn B in each of next 4 sc, 1 sc in Yarn C in next sc, 2 sc in Yarn C in next sc, 1 sc in Yarn B in each of next 4 sc*; rep * to * 7 more times = 88 sc.

Cut Yarns A and C. Continue in Yarn B.

Rnd 12: *2 sc in next sc, 1 sc in each of next 10 sc*; rep * to * 7 more times = 96 sc.

Rnd 13: *1 sc in each of next 4 sc, 2 sc in next sc, 1 sc in each of next 7 sc*; rep * to * 7 more times (with last yarnover in Yarn A) = 104 sc.

Cut Yarn B. Continue in Yarns A and C.

Rnd 14: *1 sc in Yarn A in each of next 2 sc, 1 sc in Yarn C in each of next 2 sc, 2 sc in Yarn A in next sc, 1 sc in Yarn C in each of next 2 sc, 1 sc in Yarn A in each of next 2 sc, 2 sc in Yarn C in next sc, 1 sc in Yarn A in each of next 2 sc, 2 sc in Yarn C in next sc*; rep * to * 7 more times and end with 1 sl st in Yarn A in the 1st sc = 128 sc.

Rnd 15: 1 sc in Yarn A in each sc in Yarn A and 1 sc in Yarn C in each sc in Yarn C, ending with 1 sl st in Yarn A in the 1st sc.

Rnds 16 and 17: Work as for Rnd 15.

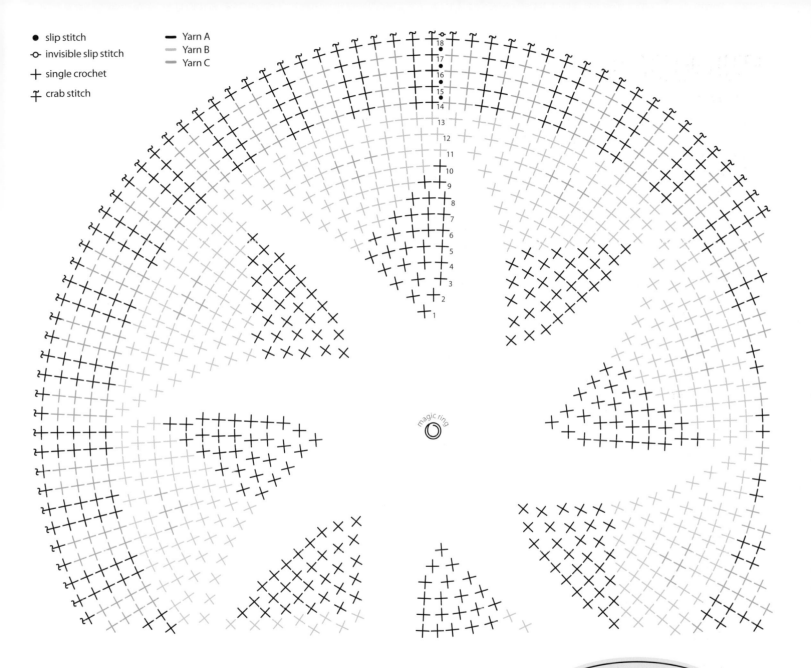

Legend:
- ● slip stitch
- ○ invisible slip stitch
- + single crochet
- ‡ crab stitch

- — Yarn A
- — Yarn B
- — Yarn C

magic ring

Cut Yarn C. Continue in Yarn A.

Rnd 18: Work crab stitch around (= single crochet worked clockwise instead of counterclockwise), cut yarn, and end with 1 invisible sl st in the 1st sc.

Weave in ends. Block the work (see page 13) and let dry completely. Attach metal ring to last rnd at the top of a line of black stitches, then thread necklace cord through ring.

Bonus idea

Decorate the pendant even more by gluing a rhinestone or other craft jewel to the center or stringing a simpler pendant or large teardrop sequin onto the necklace cord on either side of the mandala pendant.

MINI-MANDALA BUNTING

photos page 64

MATERIALS	Length: about 5 ft, 10¾ in / 180 cm	Difficulty: simple

Leftover yarns of similar weights and your choice of colors; the bunting pictured was made with small amounts of CYCA #1 (sock/fingering/baby) DMC Natura Just Cotton (100% combed cotton; 170 yd/155 m / 50 g) in Rose Layette N06, Gris Argent N09, Light Green N12, Coral N18, Aquamarine N25, Forest Green N46, Chartreuse N48, Erica N51, Plum N59, and Prussian N64

10 tassels, 1½ in / 4 cm long, in various colors

Sewing thread in matching colors

Crochet hooks, U.S. size C-2/D-3 / 3 mm and U.S. size 7 / 4.5 mm

For finishing: tapestry needle, sewing kit

Note

The bunting is made with twenty mini-mandalas: ten that are tricolored and ten that are bicolored. Mix and match the colors however you like!

TRICOLORED MINI-MANDALAS

With smaller hook and Yarn A, make a magic ring.

Rnd 1: 8 sc into ring, 1 sl st in the 1st sc. Tighten ring.

Rnd 2: Ch 1, 2 sc in each sc around, cut yarn, and end with 1 invisible sl st in the 1st sc = 16 sc.

Rnd 3: With Yarn B, work 1 standing sc into any sc, *[1 hdc (worked very loose and long) into center of ring, skip 1 sc], 1 sc in next sc*; rep * to * 6 more times, rep within brackets once more, cut yarn, and end with 1 invisible sl st in the standing sc = 16 sts.

Rnd 4: With Yarn C, work 1 standing dc into any st, ch 1, *1 dc in next st, ch 1*; rep * to * around, cut yarn, and end with 1 invisible sl st in the standing dc = 32 sts.

Rnd 5: With Yarn A, work 1 standing sc and 2 sc around a ch, 3 sc around each ch around, cut yarn, and end with 1 invisible sl st in the standing sc = 48 sc.

Work 9 more tricolored mini-mandalas the same way. Weave in ends. Sew a tassel to the lower edge of each mini-mandala.

BICOLORED MINI-MANDALAS

With smaller hook and Yarn A, make a magic ring.

Rnd 1: Ch 3 (= 1 dc), 9 dc into ring and end with 1 sl st in the 3rd ch = 10 dc.

Rnd 2: Ch 3 (= 1 dc), 1 dc into the base of these 3 ch, 2 dc in each dc around, and end with 1 sl st in the 3rd ch = 20 dc.

Rnd 3: Ch 3 (= 1 dc), 2 dc in the 1st dc, *1 dc in next dc, 2 dc in next dc*; rep * to * 8 more times, cut yarn, and end with 1 invisible sl st in the 3rd ch = 30 dc.

Rnd 4: With Yarn B, work 1 standing sc and 1 sc into any dc, 2 sc in each dc around, cut yarn, and end with 1 invisible sl st in the standing sc = 60 sc.

Work 9 more biocolored mini-mandalas the same way. Weave in ends.

BUNTING

With larger hook and yarn held double, ch 10, 1 sl st in the 1st ch (= 1st hanging loop), *ch 15, 2 sc into top of a tricolored mini-mandala, ch 15, 2 sc into top of a bicolored mini-mandala*; rep * to * 9 more times, ch 25, skip 9 ch, and end with 1 sl st into the 10th ch (= 2nd hanging loop), cut yarn and tie off.

Weave in ends.

Tricolored mini-mandala

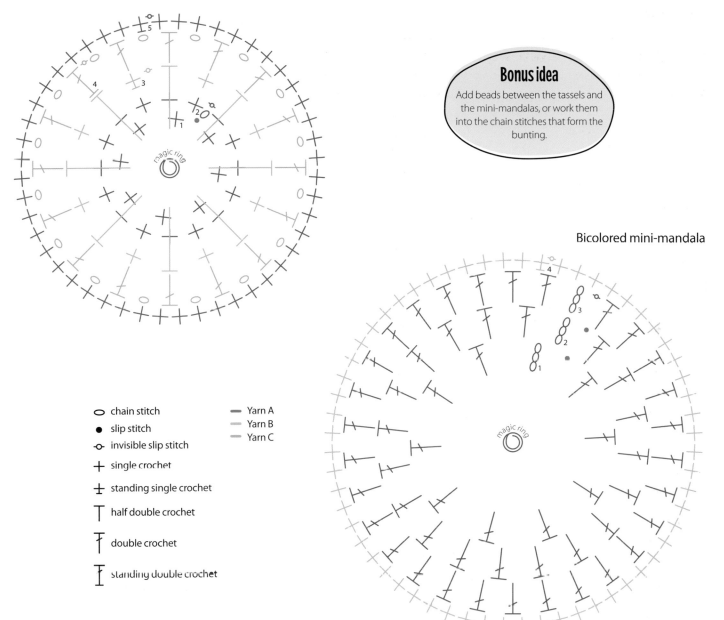

Bicolored mini-mandala

Bonus idea

Add beads between the tassels and the mini-mandalas, or work them into the chain stitches that form the bunting.

⊙ chain stitch

● slip stitch

⊶ invisible slip stitch

+ single crochet

+ standing single crochet

T half double crochet

T double crochet

I standing double crochet

— Yarn A

— Yarn B

— Yarn C

RAKU-INSPIRED TABLE MAT

photo page 65 – charts pages 79, 81 and 83

MATERIALS	Diameter after blocking: 21 in / 53.5 cm	Difficulty: expert
CYCA #1 (sock/fingering/baby) PurPle Laines Chinée (100% wool; 32 yd/29 m / 10 g): 220 g of Black (A); 15 g each of Pastel (D) and Cobalt Blue (E); 10 g each of Confetti Pink (B), Sky Blue (C), and Red Sky (F) CYCA #1 (sock/fingering/baby) PurPle Laines	Alpaca (100% alpaca; 213 yd/195 m / 50 g): 5 g of Fuchsia (G) Crochet hook, U.S. size H-8 / 5 mm For finishing: tapestry needle, pair of scissors, tailor's chalk, basin of water, blocking mat (or other surface), pins, drawing compass	

This project is worked with the yarn held double: Take the yarn end on the outside of the skein and the yarn end from the center, and work both held together.

The pattern is done with tapestry crochet—carry the unused yarns along the back of the work and swap in as necessary for color changes (see page 11). To keep all parts of the work the same thickness, on rounds without color changes you should still catch Yarn A held double inside stitches.

After cutting yarn, remember to start new colors or rounds at a variety of points around the edge of the work, to disguise increases and to help the work stay as circular as possible.

Tip

Use a stitch marker to help you keep track of where new rounds begin. Count stitches at the end of each round to make sure you've worked the round correctly.

Note: *Sections with color changes should not include increases.*

With Yarn A held double, make a magic ring.

Rnd 1: 6 sc into ring and end with 1 sl st in the 1st sc. Tighten ring.

Rnd 2: Begin catching Yarn A held double inside stitches. Ch 1, 2 sc in each sc around, and end with 1 sl st in the 1st sc = 12 sc.

Rnd 3: Ch 1, *1 sc in next sc, 2 sc in next sc*; rep * to * 5 more times, cut working yarn, and end with 1 invisible sl st in the 1st sc = 18 sc. Cut doubled Yarn A inside stitches, too, flush with surface of work.

Rnd 4: Start working with Yarn A held double in any sc, and catch Yarn A held double inside stitches, too. Ch 1, 1 sc in sc where you began working, 1 sc in next sc, 2 sc in next sc, *1 sc in each of next 2 sc, 2 sc in next sc*; rep * to * 4 more times and end with 1 sl st in the 1st sc = 24 sc.

Rnd 5: Ch 1, *1 sc in each of next 3 sc, 2 sc in next sc*; rep * to * 5 more times, cut working yarns, and end with 1 invisible sl st in the 1st sc = 30 sc. Cut doubled Yarn A inside sts as before.

Rnd 6: Start working with Yarn A held double in any sc, and catch Yarn A held double inside stitches, too. Ch 1, 1 sc in sc where you began working, 1 sc in each of next 3 sc, 2 sc in next sc, *1 sc in each of next 4 sc, 2 sc in next sc*; rep * to * 4 more times and end with 1 sl st in the 1st sc = 36 sts.

Rnd 7: Ch 1, *1 sc in each of next 5 sc, 2 sc in next sc*; rep * to * 5 more times, cut working yarns, and end with 1 invisible sl st in the 1st sc = 42 sc. Cut doubled Yarn A inside sts as before.

Rnd 8: Start working with Yarn B held double in any sc, and catch Yarn A held double inside stitches to use for color changes. Ch 1 with B, 1 sc with B in sc where you began working, 1 sc with B in each of next 5 sc, 1 sc with B and 1 sc with A in next sc, *1 sc with A in each of next 6 sc, 2 sc with A in next sc*; rep * to * 4 more times (with last yarnover of last sc in Yarn B), and end with 1 sl st with B in the 1st sc = 48 sc.

Rnd 9: Ch 1 with B, 1 sc with B in each of next 7 sc, 2 sc with A in next sc, *1 sc with A in each of next 7 sc, 2 sc with A in next sc*; rep * to * 4 more times (with last yarnover of last sc in Yarn B), cut yarns, and end with 1 invisible sl st with B in the 1st sc = 54 sc.

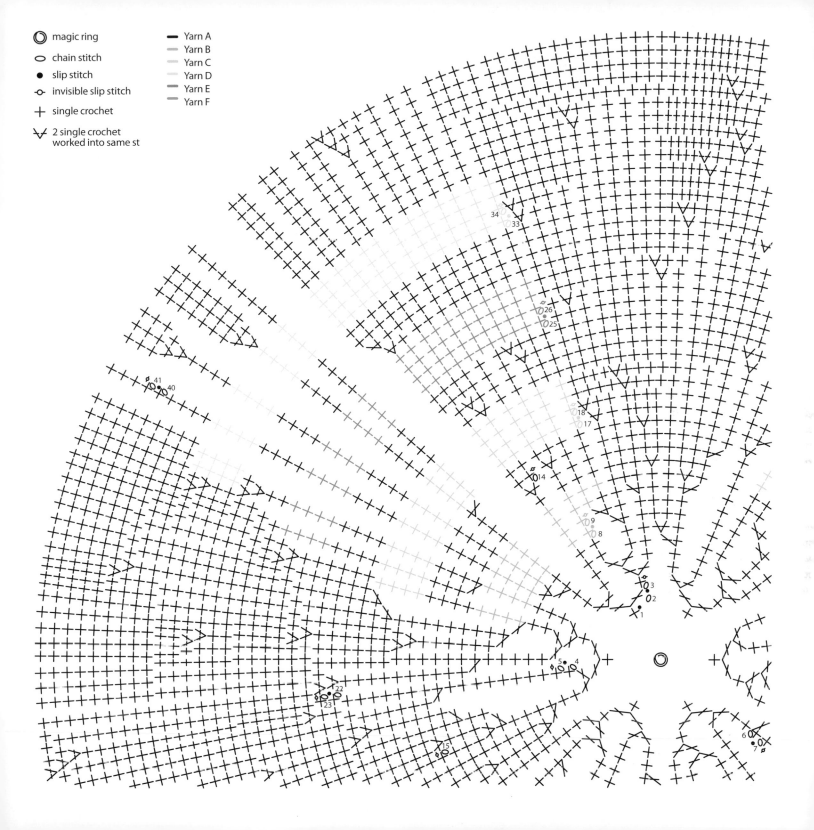

Legend

- ◎ magic ring
- ○ chain stitch
- ● slip stitch
- ⊸ invisible slip stitch
- + single crochet
- ⋎ 2 single crochet worked into same st

- ── Yarn A
- ── Yarn B
- ── Yarn C
- ── Yarn D
- ── Yarn E
- ── Yarn F

Rnd 10: Start working with Yarn A held double in any sc worked with A; catch Yarn B held double inside stitches to use for color changes. Ch 1 with A, 1 sc with A in sc where you began working, 1 sc with A in each of next 7 sc, 2 sc with A in next sc, *1 sc with A in each of next 8 sc, 2 sc with A in next sc*; rep * to * 4 more times, working 1 sc with B in the sc with A preceding the motif and 1 sc with B in each of next 7 sc with B (delaying an increase if necessary), and ending with 1 sl st with A in the 1st sc = 60 sc.

Rnd 11: Ch 1 with A, *1 sc with A in each of next 9 sc, 2 sc with A in next sc*; rep * to * 5 more times, working 1 sc with B in the sc with A preceding the motif and 1 sc with B in each of next 7 sc with B (delaying an increase if necessary). Cut Yarn A and end with 1 invisible sl st with A in the 1st sc = 66 sc. Cut doubled Yarn B inside stitches, too, flush with surface of work.

Rnd 12: Skip 43 sc after last sc with B, and start working with Yarn C held double in next sc; catch Yarn A held double inside stitches to use for color changes. Ch 1 with C, 1 sc with C in the sc where you began working, 1 sc with C in each of next 4 sc, 1 sc with A in each of next 5 sc, 2 sc with A in next sc, *1 sc with A in each of next 10 sc, 2 sc with A in next sc*; rep * to * 3 more times, 1 sc with A in each of next 5 sc, 2 sc with A in next sc, 1 sc with C in each of last 5 sc, and end with 1 sl st with C in the 1st sc = 72 sc.

Rnd 13: Ch 1 with C, 1 sc with C in each of next 5 sc, 1 sc with A in next sc, 2 sc with A in next sc, *1 sc with A in each of next 11 sc, 2 sc with A in next sc*; rep * to * 4 more times, 1 sc with C in each of last 5 sc, cut Yarn C, and end with 1 invisible sl st with C in the 1st sc = 78 sc.

Cut doubled Yarn A inside stitches, too, flush with surface of work.

Rnd 14: Start working with Yarn A held double in any sc with A; catch Yarn C held double inside stitches to use for color changes. Ch 1 with A, 1 sc with A in the sc where you began working, 1 sc with A in each of next 11 sc, 2 sc with A in next sc, *1 sc with A in each of next 12 sc, 2 sc with A in next sc*; rep * to * 4 more times, working 1 sc with C in the sc with A preceding the motif in Yarn C and 1 sc with C in each of next 10 sc with C (delaying an increase if necessary). Cut Yarn A and end with 1 invisible sl st with A in the 1st sc = 84 sts. Cut doubled Yarn C inside stitches, too, flush with surface of work.

Rnd 15: Start working with Yarn A held double in any sc with A; catch Yarn C held double inside stitches to use for color changes. Ch 1 with A, 1 sc with A in the sc where you began working, 1 sc with A in each of next 12 sc, 2 sc with A in next sc, *1 sc with A in each of next 13 sc, 2 sc with A in next sc*; rep * to * 4 more times, working 1 sc with C in each of 11 sc with C (delaying an increase if necessary). Cut Yarn A and end with 1 invisible sl st with A in the 1st sc = 90 sts. Cut doubled Yarn C inside stitches, too, flush with surface of work.

Rnd 16: Skip 14 sc after the last sc with C and start working with Yarn C held double in next sc; catch Yarn A held double inside stitches to use for color changes. Ch 1 with C, 1 sc with C in the sc where you began working, 1 sc with C in each of next 12 sc, 1 sc with A in next sc, 2 sc with A in next sc, *1 sc with A in each of next 14 sc, 2 sc with A in next sc*; rep * to * 4 more times (with last yarnover of last sc in Yarn C), and end with 1 sl st with C in the 1st sc = 96 sc.

Rnd 17: Ch 1 with C, 1 sc with C in each of next 13 sc, 1 sc with A in each of next 2 sc, 2 sc with A in next sc, *1 sc with A in each of next 15 sc, 2 sc with A in next sc*; rep * to * 4 more times, cut yarn, and end with 1 invisible sl st with C in the 1st sc = 102 sc.

Rnd 18: Start working with Yarn A held double in any sc with A; catch Yarn C held double inside stitches to use for color changes. Ch 1 with A, 1 sc with A in the sc where you began working, 1 sc with A in each of next 15 sc, 2 sc with A in next sc, *1 sc with A in each of next 16 sc, 2 sc with A in next sc*; rep * to * 4 more times, working 1 sc with C in each of the 13 sc with C of prev rnd (delaying an increase if necessary), and end with 1 sl st with A in the 1st sc = 108 sc.

Rnd 19: Ch 1 with A, *1 sc with A in each of next 17 sc, 2 sc with A in next sc*; rep * to * 5 more times, working 1 sc with C in each of the 13 sc with C of prev rnd (delaying an increase if necessary). Cut Yarn A and end with 1 invisible sl st with A in the 1st sc = 114 sc. Cut doubled Yarn C inside stitches, too, flush with surface of work.

Rnd 20: Start working with Yarn D held double in the sc situated vertically in line with the right-hand edge of the 1st motif in Yarn C; catch Yarn A held double inside stitches to use for color changes. Ch 1 with D, 1 sc with D in the sc where you began working, 1 sc with D in each of next 13 sc, 1 sc with A in each of next 4 sc, 2 sc with A in next sc, *1 sc with A in each of next 18 sc, 2 sc with A in next sc*; rep * to * 4 more times (with last yarnover of last sc in Yarn D), and end with 1 sl st with D in the 1st sc = 120 sc.

Rnd 21: Ch 1 with D, 1 sc with D in each of next 14 sc, 1 sc with A in each of next 5 sc, 2 sc

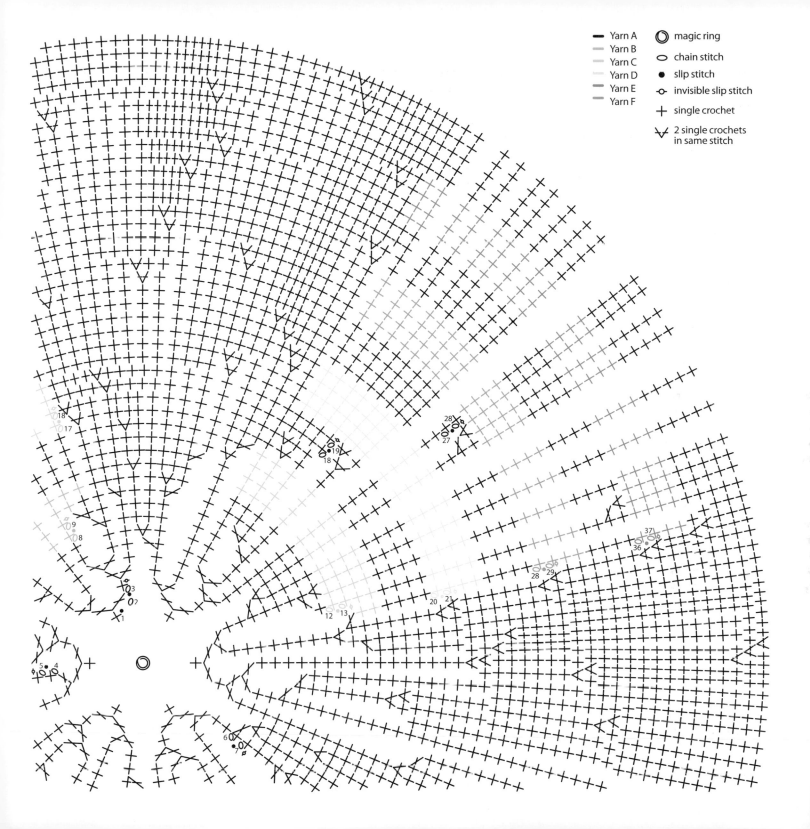

Tip

The yarn caught inside the stitches and the color changes will probably tighten the work a little—it may be a good idea to stretch it now and then as you go along.

with A in next sc, *1 sc with A in each of next 19 sc, 2 sc with A in next sc*; rep * to * 4 more times (with last yarnover of last sc in Yarn D), cut yarn, and end with 1 invisible sl st with D in the 1st sc = 126 sts.

Rnd 22: Start working with Yarn A held double in any sc with A; catch Yarn D held double inside stitches to use for color changes. Ch 1 with A, 1 sc with A in the sc where you began working, 1 sc with A in each of next 19 sc, 2 sc with A in next sc, *1 sc with A in each of next 20 sc, 2 sc with A in next sc*; rep * to * 4 more times, working 1 sc with D in each of the 14 sc with D (delaying an increase if necessary), and end with 1 sl st with A in the 1st sc = 132 sc.

Rnd 23: Ch 1 with A, *1 sc with A in each of next 21 sc, 2 sc with A in next sc*; rep * to * 5 more times, working 1 sc with D in each of the 14 sc with D (delaying an increase if necessary). Cut Yarn A and end with 1 invisible sl st with A in the 1st sc = 138 sc. Cut doubled Yarn D inside stitches, too, flush with surface of work.

Rnd 24: Start working with Yarn E held double in the sc situated vertically in line with the right-hand edge of the 2nd motif in Yarn C; catch Yarn A held double inside stitches to use for color changes. Ch 1 with E, 1 sc with E in the sc where you began working, 1 sc with E in each of next 16 sc, 1 sc with A in each of next 5 sc, 2 sc with A in next sc, *1 sc with A in each of next 22 sc, 2 sc with A in next sc*; rep * to * 4 more times (with last yarnover of last sc in Yarn E), and end with 1 sl st with E in the 1st sc = 144 sc.

Rnd 25: Ch 1 with E, 1 sc with E in each of next 17 sc, 1 sc with A in each of next 6 sc, 2 sc with A in next sc, *1 sc with A in each of next 23 sc, 2 sc with A in next sc*; rep * to * 4 more times (with last yarnover of last sc in Yarn E), cut yarn, and end with 1 invisible sl st with E in the 1st sc = 150 sc.

Rnd 26: Start working with Yarn A held double in any sc with A; catch Yarn E held double inside stitches to use for color changes. Ch 1 with A, 1 sc with A in the sc where you began working, 1 sc with A in each of next 23 sc, 2 sc with A in next sc, *1 sc with A in each of next 24 sc, 2 sc with A in next sc*; rep * to * 4 more times, working 1 sc with E in each of the 17 sc with E (delaying an increase if necessary), and end with 1 sl st with A in the 1st sc = 156 sc.

Rnd 27: Ch 1 with A, *1 sc with A in each of next 25 sc, 2 sc with A in next sc*; rep * to * 5 more times, working 1 sc with E in each of the 17 sc with E (delaying an increase if necessary). Cut Yarn A and end with 1 invisible sl st with A in the 1st sc = 162 sc. Cut doubled Yarn E inside stitches, too, flush with surface of work.

Rnd 28: Start working with Yarn F held double in the sc situated vertically in line with the righthand edge of the motif in Yarn D; catch Yarn A held double inside stitches to use for color changes. Ch 1 with F, 1 sc with F in the sc where you began working, 1 sc with F in each of next 16 sc, 1 sc with A in each of next 9 sc, 2 sc with A in next sc, *1 sc with A in each of next 26 sc, 2 sc with A in next sc*; rep * to * 4 more times (with last yarnover of last sc in Yarn E), 1 sl st with F in the 1st sc = 168 sc.

Rnd 29: Ch 1 with F, 1 sc with F in each of next 17 sc, 1 sc with A in each of next 10 sc, 2 sc with A in next sc, *1 sc with A in each of next 27 sc, 2 sc with A in next sc*; rep * to * 4 more times (with last yarnover of last sc in Yarn E), cut yarn, and end with 1 invisible sl st with F in the 1st sc = 174 sc.

Rnd 30: Start working with Yarn A held double in any sc with A; catch Yarn F held double inside stitches to use for color changes. Ch 1 with A, 1 sc with A in the sc where you began working, 1 sc with A in each of next 27 sc, 2 sc with A in next sc, *1 sc with A in each of next 28 sc, 2 sc with A in next sc*; rep * to * 4 more times, working 1 sc with F in each of 17 sc with F (delaying an increase if necessary), and end with 1 sl st with A in the 1st sc = 180 sc.

Rnd 31: Ch 1 with A, *1 sc with A in each of next 29 sc, 2 sc with A in next sc*; rep * to * 5 more times, working 1 sc with F in each of 17 sc with F (delaying an increase if necessary), cut Yarn A, and end with 1 invisible sl st with A in the 1st sc = 186 sc. Cut doubled Yarn F inside stitches, too, flush with surface of work.

Rnd 32: Start working with Yarn D held double in the sc situated vertically in line with the right-hand edge of the motif in Yarn E; catch Yarn A held double inside stitches to use for color changes. Ch 1 with D, 1 sc with D in

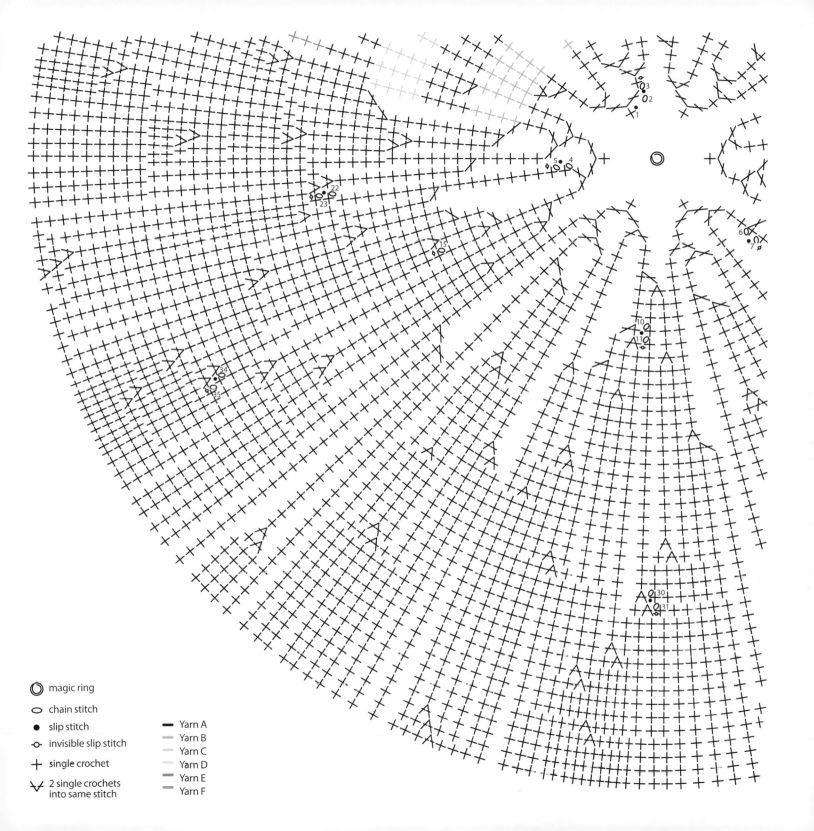

the sc where you began working, 1 sc with D in each of next 18 sc, 1 sc with A in each of next 11 sc, 2 sc with A in next sc, *1 sc with A in each of 30 next sc, 2 sc with A in next sc*; rep * to * 4 more times (with last yarnover of last sc in Yarn D), and end with 1 sl st with D in the 1st sc = 192 sc.

Rnd 33: Ch 1 with A, 1 sc with D in each of next 19 sc, 1 sc with A in each of next 12 sc, 2 sc with A in next sc, *1 sc with A in each of next 31 sc, 2 sc with A in next sc*; rep * to * 4 more times (with last yarnover of last sc in Yarn D), cut Yarn A, and end with 1 invisible sl st with A in the 1st sc =198 sc. Cut doubled Yarn D inside stitches, too, flush with surface of work.

Rnd 34: Start working with Yarn A held double in any sc with A; catch Yarn D held double inside stitches to use for color changes. Ch 1 with A, 1 sc with A in the sc where you began working, 1 sc with A in each of 31 next sc, 2 sc with A in next sc, *1 sc with A in each of next 32 sc, 2 sc with A in next sc*; rep * to * 4 more times, working 1 sc with D in each of 19 sc with D (delaying an increase if necessary), and end with 1 sl st with A in the 1st sc = 204 sc.

Rnd 35: Ch 1 with A, *1 sc with A in each of next 33 sc, 2 sc with A in next sc*; rep * to * 5 more times, working 1 sc with D in each of 19 sc with D (delaying an increase if necessary). Cut Yarn A and end with 1 invisible sl st with A in the 1st sc = 210 sc. Cut doubled Yarn D inside stitches, too, flush with surface of work.

Rnd 36: Start working with Yarn E held double in the sc situated vertically in line with the right-hand edge of the motif in Yarn F; catch

Yarn A held double inside stitches to use for color changes. Ch 1 with E, 1 sc with E in the sc where you began working, 1 sc with E in each of next 19 sc, 1 sc with A in each of next 14 sc, 2 sc with A in next sc, *1 sc with A in each of next 34 sc, 2 sc with A in next sc*; rep * to * 4 more times (with last yarnover of last sc in Yarn E), and end with 1 sl st with E in the 1st sc = 216 sc.

Rnd 37: Ch 1 with E, 1 sc with E in each of next 20 sc, 1 sc with A in each of next 15 sc, 2 sc with A in next sc, *1 sc with A in each of next 35 sc, 2 sc with A in next sc*; rep * to * 4 more times (with last yarnover of last sc in Yarn E), cut yarn, and end with 1 invisible sl st with E in the 1st sc = 222 sc.

Rnd 38: Start working with Yarn A held double in any sc with A; catch Yarn E held double inside stitches to use for color changes. Ch 1 with A, 1 sc with A in the sc where you began working, 1 sc with A in each of next 35 sc, 2 sc with A in next sc, *1 sc with A in each of next 36 sc, 2 sc with A in next sc*; rep * to * 4 more times, working 1 sc with E in each of 20 sc with E (delaying an increase if necessary), and end with 1 sl st with A in the 1st sc = 228 sc.

Rnd 39: Ch 1 with A, *1 sc with A in each of next 37 sc, 2 sc with A in next sc*; rep * to * 5 more times, working 1 sc with E in each of 20 sc with E (delaying an increase if necessary). Cut Yarn A and end with 1 invisible sl st with A in the 1st sc = 234 sc. Cut doubled Yarn E inside stitches, too, flush with surface of work.

Rnd 40: Start working with Yarn A held double in any sc; catch Yarn A held double inside stitches to maintain thickness of work.

Ch 1, 1 sc in the sc where you began working, 1 sc in each of next 37 sc, 2 sc in next sc, *1 sc in each of next 38 sc, 2 sc in next sc*; rep * to * 4 more times and end with 1 sl st in the 1st sc = 240 sc.

Rnd 41: Ch 1, *1 sc in each of next 39 sc, 2 sc in next sc*; rep * to * 5 more times, cut yarn, and end with 1 invisible sl st in the 1st sc = 246 sc. Cut doubled Yarn A inside stitches, too, flush with surface of work.

Rnd 42: Start working with Yarn A held double in any sc; catch Yarn A held double inside stitches to maintain thickness of work. Ch 1, 1 sc in the sc where you began working, 1 sc in each of next 39 sc, 2 sc in next sc, *1 sc in each of next 40 sc, 2 sc in next sc*; rep * to * 4 more times and end with 1 sl st in the 1st sc = 252 sc.

Rnd 43: Ch 1, *1 sc in each of 41 next sc, 2 sc in next sc*; rep * to * 5 more times and end with 1 sl st in the 1st sc = 258 sc.

Rnd 44: Ch 1, *1 sc in each of next 42 sc, 2 sc in next sc*; rep * to * 5 more times, cut yarn, and end with 1 invisible sl st in the 1st sc = 264 sc. Cut doubled Yarn A inside stitches, too, flush with surface of work.

Weave in ends. If any are poking out on RS of work, use a needle to shove them back to WS. Block the work (see page 13). With tailor's chalk, mark outlines for 3 circles (about 1¾ in / 4.5 cm, 3 in / 7.5 cm, and 5½ in / 14 cm in diameter; see photo on page 65). Embroider over these outlines in backstitch with Yarn G held double.

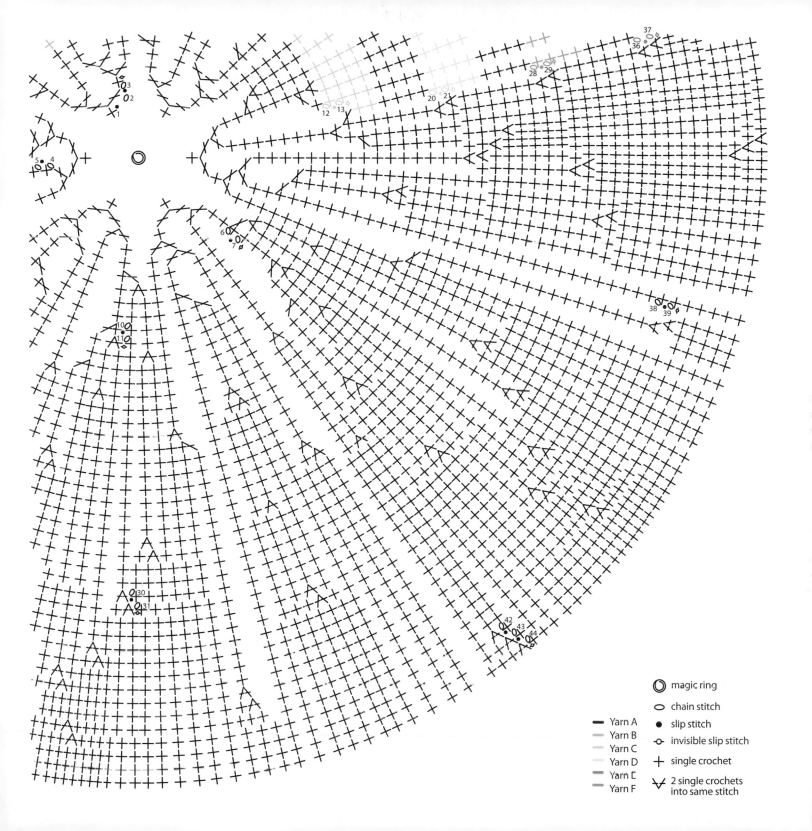

magic ring

chain stitch

slip stitch

invisible slip stitch

single crochet

2 single crochets
into same stitch

— Yarn A
— Yarn B
— Yarn C
— Yarn D
— Yarn E
— Yarn F

COASTERS

photo page 66

MATERIALS	Diameter: 5 in / 13 cm	Difficulty: simple
CYCA #1 (sock/fingering/baby) DMC Natura Just Cotton (100% combed cotton; 170 yd/155 m / 50 g), 50 g of Linen N78 (A1); 15 m of each of the following colors (B): Crimson N61, Prussian N64, Moss Green N75, Plum N59, Chartreuse N48, Coral N18	CYCA #0 (lace/fingering) DMC Cebelia Cotton size 30 (100% mercerized cotton; 567 yd/518 m / 50 g), CYCA #0 (lace/fingering): 50 g of Ecru (A2) Crochet hook, U.S. size E-4 / 3.5 mm For finishing: tapestry needle, pair of scissors, iron	

Bonus idea
Use a stitch marker to make it easy to find the beginning of each round (see page 6).

Note
The pattern is worked in tapestry crochet—carry the unused yarns along the back of the work and swap in as necessary for color changes (see page 11).

For main color, Yarns A1 and A2 held together = "Yarn A."

With Yarn A, make a magic ring.

Rnd 1: 8 sc into ring, and end with 1 sl st in the 1st sc. Tighten ring.

Rnd 2: Ch 1, *1 sc in each of next 2 sc, 2 sc in next sc*; rep * to * once more,
1 sc in each of last 2 sc, and end with 1 sl st in the 1st sc = 10 sc.

Rnd 3: Ch 1, *1 sc in each of next 2 sc, 2 sc in next sc*; rep * to * 2 more times, 2 sc in last sc, and end with 1 sl st in the 1st sc = 14 sc.

Rnd 4: Ch 1, *1 sc in next sc, 2 sc in next sc*; rep * to * around and end with 1 sl st in the 1st sc = 21 sc.

Rnd 5: Ch 1, *1 sc in next sc, 2 sc in next sc*; rep * to * around until 1 sc rem, 1 sc in last sc, and end with 1 sl st in the 1st sc = 31 sc.

Rnd 6: Work as for Rnd 5 = 46 sc.

Rnds 7-9: Ch 1, sc around and end with 1 sl st in the 1st sc.

Rnd 10: Work as for Rnd 4 = 69 sc.

Rnd 11: Move Yarn A to back of work and carry as you go. With Yarn B, ch 1, 1 sc in each of first 2 sc, 2 sc in next sc, 1 sc in each rem sc around, and end with 1 sl st in the 1st sc = 70 sc.

Rnd 12: Ch 1 with B, *1 sc with B in each of next 5 sc, 1 sc with A in each of next 2 sc*; rep * to * around and end with 1 sl st with A in the 1st sc.

Rnd 13: Ch 1 with A, 1 sc with A in the 1st sc, *[1 sc with B in each of next 3 sc, 1 sc with A in next sc, 2 sc with A in each of next 2 sc], 1 sc with A in next sc*; rep * to * 8 more times, rep within brackets once more, and end with 1 sl st with A in the 1st sc = 90 sc.

Rnd 14: Ch 1 with A, 1 sc with A in each of first 2 sc, *1 sc with B in next sc, 1 sc with A in each of next 8 sc*; rep * to * 8 more times, 1 sc with B in next sc, 1 sc with A in each of last 6 sc, and end with 1 sl st with A in the 1st sc. Cut Yarn B and continue in Yarn A.

Rnd 15: Ch 1, 1 sc in each of first 2 sc, *2 sc in next sc, 1 sc in each of next 8 sc*; rep * to * 8 more times, 2 sc in next sc, 1 sc in each of last 6 sc, and end with 1 sl st in the 1st sc = 100 sc. Cut yarn and fasten off.

Weave in ends. Work 5 more coasters the same way, using a different color for Yarn B each time. Steam press coasters gently on wrong sides only.

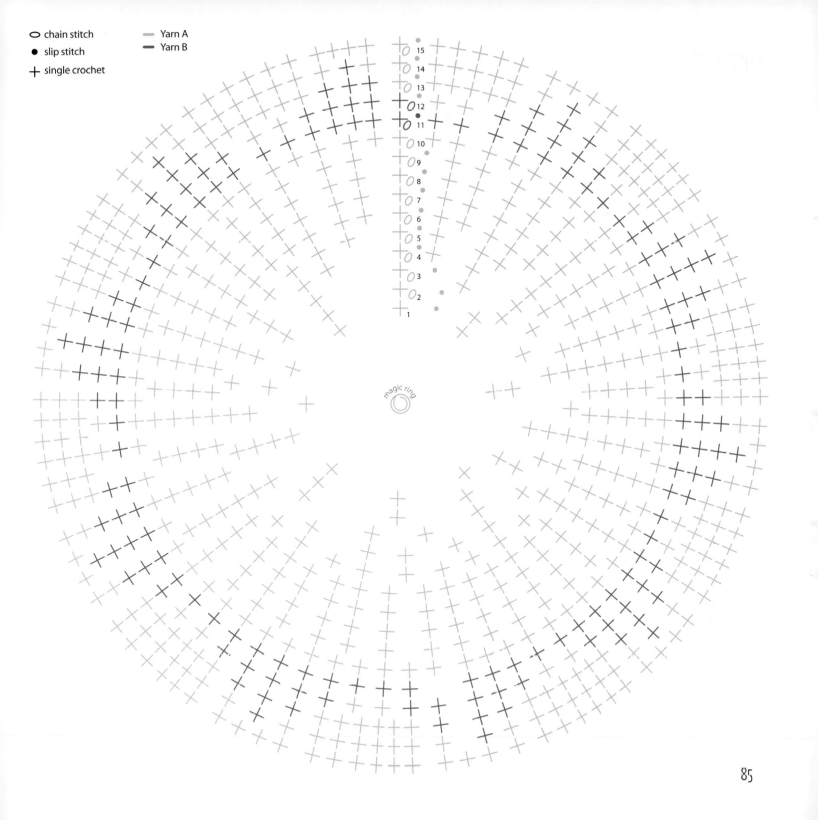

chain stitch
slip stitch
single crochet

Yarn A
Yarn B

85

DESERT CARPET

photo page 67

MATERIALS	Diameter: 43¼ in / 110 cm	Difficulty: simple
CYCA #5 (chunky/craft/rug) DMC Natura XL Just Cotton (100% cotton; 82 yd/75 m / 100 g), 500 g of Curry 92 (B); 400 g each of Beige 31 (D) and Ecru 03 (E); 300 g each of Brown 11 (A) and Taupe 32 (C)	Crochet hook, U.S. size M/N-13 / 9 mm For finishing: tapestry needle, pair of scissors	

This pattern is worked with two yarns held together throughout. Sometimes the yarns will be two different colors, but sometimes they'll be the same, in which case you can pull from the outside and the center of the same skein.

Remember to start new colors or rounds at a variety of points around the edge of the work to help the work stay as circular as possible.

With 2 strands of Yarn A held together, make a magic ring.

Rnd 1: Ch 3 (= 1 dc), 11 dc into ring and end with 1 sl st in the 3rd ch = 12 dc. Tighten ring.

Rnd 2: Ch 3 (= 1 dc), 1 dc into the base of these 3 ch, 2 dc into each dc around, cut yarns, and end with 1 invisible sl st in the 3rd ch = 24 dc.

Rnd 3: With 1 strand of Yarn A and 1 strand of Yarn B held together, ch 3 (= 1 dc). 2 dc in next dc, *1 dc in next dc, 2 dc in next dc*; rep * to * around and end with 1 sl st in the 3rd ch = 36 dc.

Rnd 4: Ch 3 (= 1 dc), 1 dc in next dc, 2 dc in next dc, *1 dc in each of next 2 dc, 2 dc in next dc*; rep * to * around, cut yarns, and end with 1 invisible sl st in the 3rd ch = 48 dc.

Rnd 5: With 2 strands of Yarn B held together, ch 3 (= 1 dc). 1 dc in each of next 2 dc, 2 dc in next dc, *1 dc in each of next 3 dc, 2 dc in next dc*; rep * to * around and end with 1 sl st in the 3rd ch = 60 dc.

Continue increasing 12 dc each rnd, adding 1 dc between increases each time (table on facing page summarizes these increases).

When you have completed all increases, cut yarns, fasten off, and weave in ends.

Tip

To help keep the work as circular as possible, you can introduce new yarns with a standing double crochet (see page 10) instead of 3 chain stitches.

Round	Yarns	Double crochets between increases	Total sts
1	A + A	–	12
2	A + A	0	24
3	A + B	1	36
4	A + B	2	48
5	B + B	3	60
6	B + B	4	72
7	B + C	5	84
8	B + C	6	96
9	C + C	7	108
10	C + C	8	120
11	C + D	9	132
12	C + D	10	144
13	D + D	11	156
14	D + D	12	168
15	D + E	13	180
16	D + E	14	192
17	E + E	15	204
18	E + E	16	216
19	E + B	17	228
20	B + B	18	240
21	B + A	19	252
22	A + A	20	264

DHARMA BAG
photo page 68 - charts page 88

MATERIALS	Dimensions: 10¼ x 10¼ in / 26 x 26 cm	Difficulty: intermediate

CYCA #5 (chunky/craft/rug) DMC Natura XL Just Cotton (100% cotton; 82 yd/75 m / 100 g), 100 g of each of the following: Mint Green 07 (A), Yellow-Green 82 (B), Peach 04 (C)	1 iron-on motif, about 2¾ in / 7 cm wide
	1 zipper, at least 9½ in / 24 cm long
	47¼ in / 120 cm of chain for bag handle
colorful matching fabric, 23½ x 11¾ in / 60 x 30 cm (for bag lining)	Sewing thread: colors matching Yarns A, B and C; colors matching lining/iron-on fabric
colorful matching fabric, 4 x 4 in / 10 x 10 cm (for center of bag face beneath iron-on motif)	Crochet hook, U.S. size K-10½/L-11 / 7 mm
	For finishing: tapestry needle, sewing kit, drawing compass, iron for steam pressing

Bonus idea
This project should be worked very tightly—don't hesitate to go down a hook size. It will only look better that way!

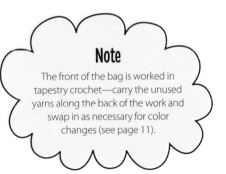

Note
The front of the bag is worked in tapestry crochet—carry the unused yarns along the back of the work and swap in as necessary for color changes (see page 11).

FRONT
With Yarn A, make a magic ring.

Rnd 1: 6 sc into ring and end with 1 sl st in the 1st sc. Tighten ring.

Rnd 2: Ch 1, 2 sc in each sc around and end with 1 sl st in the 1st sc = 12 sc.

Rnd 3: Begin carrying Yarn B and Yarn C on WS to use for color changes. With Yarn A, ch 1, *1 sc in next sc, 2 sc in next sc*; rep * to * once more with Yarn B, once more with Yarn C, once more with Yarn A, once more with Yarn B and once more with Yarn C; end with 1 sl st with A in the 1st sc = 18 sc.

Rnd 4: The round is now divided into six sections, two of each yarn color. With Yarn A, ch 1, *2 sc in the 1st sc of section, 1 sc in each sc of section until 1 sc rem, 2 sc in last sc of section*; rep * to * 5 more times, matching the working yarn color to the color of each section; end with 1 sl st with A in the 1st sc = 30 sc.

Rnd 5: With Yarn A, *1 sc in each sc of section until 1 sc rem, 2 sc in last sc of section*; rep * to * 5 more times, matching working yarn to each section as for Rnd 4; end with 1 sl st with A in the 1st sc = 36 sc.

Rnds 6-10: Rep Rnds 4 and 5 twice, and then rep Rnd 5 once more = 78 sc.

Rnd 11: Ch 1 with C; 1 sc in each sc around, but work in Yarn C over the sections done in Yarn A, in Yarn A over the sections in B, and in Yarn B over the sections in C; end with 1 sl st with C in the 1st sc.

Rnd 12: Following the same color order as in Rnd 11, work as for Rnd 5 = 84 sc.

Rnd 13: Work as for Rnd 12, ending with 1 invisible sl st (you will need to cut Yarn C) = 90 sc. Cut Yarns A and B.

PATTERN TECHNIQUE
For a neat color transition at the end of a round, work the second single crochet of the increase in the slip stitch of preceding round—this will make the slip stitch less visible.

Front

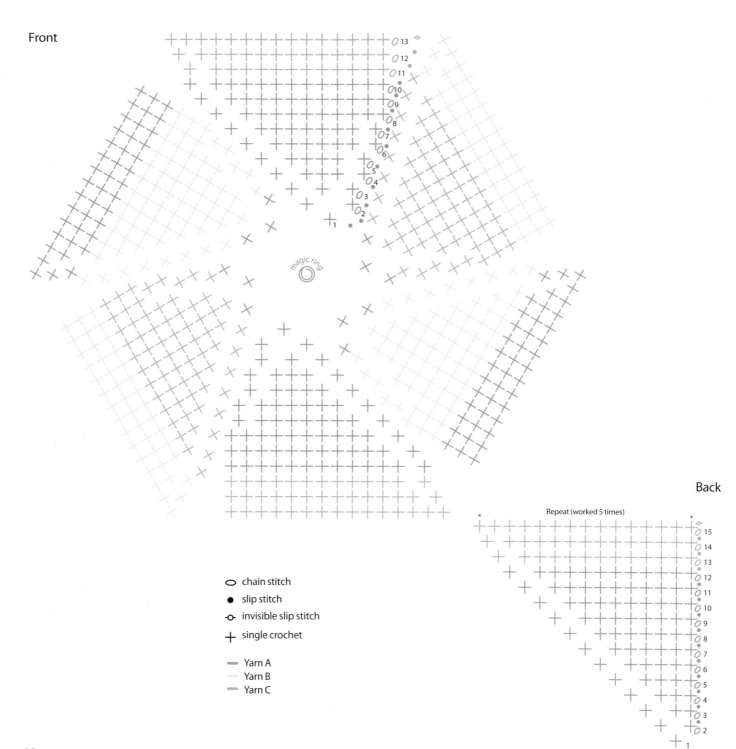

magic ring

○ chain stitch

● slip stitch

-○- invisible slip stitch

+ single crochet

— Yarn A
— Yarn B
— Yarn C

Back

Repeat (worked 5 times)

BACK

With Yarn A, make a magic ring.

Rnd 1: 6 sc into ring and end with 1 sl st in the 1st sc. Tighten ring.

Rnd 2: Ch 1, 2 sc in each sc around, and end with 1 sl st in the 1st sc = 12 sc.

Rnd 3: Ch 1, *1 sc in next sc, 2 sc in next sc*; rep * to * 5 more times and end with 1 sl st in the 1st sc = 18 sc.

Rnd 4: Ch 1, *1 sc in each of next 2 sc, 2 sc in next sc*; rep * to * 5 more times and end with 1 sl st in the 1st sc = 24 sc.

Rnd 5: Ch 1, *1 sc in each of next 3 sc, 2 sc in next sc*; rep * to * 5 more times and end with 1 sl st in the 1st sc = 30 sc.

Rnd 6: Ch 1, *1 sc in each of next 4 sc, 2 sc in next sc*; rep * to * 5 more times and end with 1 sl st in the 1st sc = 36 sc.

Rnd 7: Ch 1, *1 sc in each of next 5 sc, 2 sc in next sc*; rep * to * 5 more times and end with 1 sl st in the 1st sc = 42 sc.

Rnd 8: Ch 1, *1 sc in each of next 6 sc, 2 sc in next sc*; rep * to * 5 more times and end with 1 sl st in the 1st sc = 48 sc.

Rnd 9: Ch 1, *1 sc in each of next 7 sc, 2 sc in next sc*; rep * to * 5 more times and end with 1 sl st in the 1st sc = 54 sc.

Rnd 10: Ch 1, *1 sc in each of next 8 sc, 2 sc in next sc*; rep * to * 5 more times and end with 1 sl st in the 1st sc = 60 sc.

Rnd 11: Ch 1, *1 sc in each of next 9 sc, 2 sc in next sc*; rep * to * 5 more times and end with 1 sl st in the 1st sc = 66 sc.

Rnd 12: Ch 1, *1 sc in each of next 10 sc, 2 sc in next sc*; rep * to * 5 more times, cut yarn, and end with 1 invisible sl st in the 1st sc = 72 sc.

Rnd 13: Start working with Yarn C in the invisible sl st; ch 1, *1 sc in each of next 11 sc, 2 sc in next sc*; rep * to * 5 more times and end with 1 sl st in the 1st sc = 78 sc.

Rnd 14: Ch 1, *1 sc in each of next 12 sc, 2 sc in next sc*; rep * to * 5 more times and end with 1 sl st in the 1st sc = 84 sc.

Rnd 15: Ch 1, *1 sc in each of next 13 sc, 2 sc in next sc*; rep * to * 5 more times, cut yarn, and end with 1 invisible sl st in the 1st sc = 90 sc.

Weave in ends. With the iron, steam press front and back gently; do not press hard enough to crush stitches, and be sure to stretch out corners fully. Lay flat to cool.

Following manufacturer's instructions, affix the iron-on motif to the center of the smaller piece of fabric. Trace a circle around the motif, leaving at least 5 mm to spare on all sides. Cut this circle out of the fabric, fold the spare 5 mm over on the reverse, and go over the folded edge with the iron, being careful not to touch the iron on motif.

Pin the circle to center of front and sew it in place with slip stitch, using small stitches. Trace the basic shapes of the hexagonal front and back onto the fabric for the lining. Cut out both pieces, leaving ½ in / 1.5 cm to spare on all sides. Fold ¾ in / 2 cm over on the reverse (a little more than you left to spare, because the lining will stretch) and go over the folded edges with the iron.

Pin one side of zipper to WS of front, along two adjacent sides of hexagon, and pin other side to WS of back. Pin the fabric for lining to WS of front and back, over edges of zipper sides. Secure lining in place with small running stitches—sew over sides of zipper, too, so they are secured by lining seams. To reinforce the ends of the bag opening, add a few extra stitches going through both front and back, at either end of the bag opening, with the yarn you used for crocheting. Pin front and back with linings facing. Join with backstitch using a doubled length of sewing thread (changing the color of the thread for each section in order to match, if desired), working just under the chain formed by the upper loops of the stitches of last rounds of front and back.

Sew the ends of the chain for bag handle securely to the corners of the hexagon at either end of the bag opening.

Tip

If the zipper is too long, create an end at the desired point along the zipper's length with a series of stitches straddling the zipper teeth and then cut off the excess.

INDIAN GARDEN CUSHION

photo page 69 – charts page 93

MATERIALS	Diameter of cushion: 15¾ in / 40 cm	Difficulty: expert
CYCA #5 (chunky/craft/rug) DMC Natura XL Just Cotton (100% cotton; 82 yd/75 m / 100 g), 100 g of each of the following: Mustard 92 (A), Powder Pink 41 (B), Fuchsia 43 (C), Mint Green 07 (D) colorful matching fabric, 25½ x 25½ in / 65 x 65 cm 1 circular cushion form, 15¾ / 40 cm in diameter	Matching sewing thread Crochet hook, U.S. size K-10½/L-11 / 7 mm For finishing: tapestry needle, sewing kit, basin of water, blocking mat (or other surface), pins, drawing compass	

PATTERN STITCH

5-dc bobble

Inserting the hook into the same stitch throughout, work 5 incomplete double crochets (see page 10, Working stitches together): you'll end up with 6 loops on the hook. Wrap the yarn around the hook and pull through all 6 loops at once.

FIRST FLOWER LAYER

With Yarn A, make a magic ring.

Rnd 1: 6 sc into ring, tighten ring, cut yarn, and end with 1 invisible sl st in the 1st sc.

Rnd 2: With Yarn B, 1 standing sc in back loop only and 1 sc in back loop only in same sc, 2 sc in back loop only in each rem sc around, and end with 1 sl st into back loop only in the standing sc = 12 sc.

Rnd 3: Ch 1; *1 sc, 1 hdc and 1 dc in next sc; 1 dc, 1 hdc and 1 sc in next sc*; rep * to * 5 more times, cut yarn, and end with 1 invisible sl st in the 1st sc = 6 "petals" of 6 sts each.

Rnd 4: With Yarn A, 1 standing sc in the 2nd hdc of a petal, *1[1 hdc in front loop only in the sc situated vertically in line on Rnd 1, skip 1 sc],1 sc in each of next 5 sts*; rep * to * 4 more times, rep within brackets once more, 1 sc in each of last 4 sts, cut yarn, and end with 1 invisible sl st in the standing sc.

First flower layer

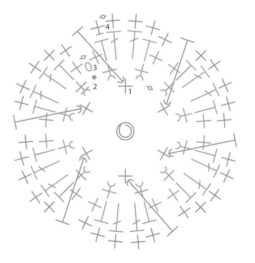

⊚ magic ring

○ chain stitch

● slip stitch

⊶ invisible slip stitch

+ single crochet

T half double crochet

Ŧ double crochet

ǐ standing stitch

Å stitch in back loop only

90

BORDER OF CENTER

Rnd 5: Turn work so WS is facing you. Working with Yarn C on WS, between 2 sc of Rnd 1: insert hook into space after 2nd sc, yoh, and pull through to WS to create a working loop on hook. *Insert hook into space after next sc and work 1 sl st very loosely*; rep * to * 5 more times. Cut yarn, thread onto tapestry needle, pull through to WS, pass through working loop, and fasten off.

SECOND FLOWER LAYER

Turn work so RS is facing you. Work behind 1st flower layer.

Rnd 6: Start working with Yarn D in any sl st on Rnd 5, on WS. Ch 5 (= 1 dc + 1 ch loop), *1 dc in next sl st, ch 2*; rep * to * 4 more times and end with 1 sl st in the 3rd ch = 6 dc and 6 ch loops.

Rnd 7: Ch 4 (= 1 dc + 1 ch), *3 dc around next ch loop, ch 1, skip 1 dc*; rep * to * 4 more times, 2 dc around last ch loop, and end with 1 sl st in the 3rd ch = 24 sts.

Rnd 8: Ch 1 (= 1 sc), *[skip 1 dc, 5 dc in next dc], skip 1 dc, 1 sc around next ch*; rep * to * 4 more times, rep within brackets once more, cut yarn, and end with 1 invisible sl st in 1st ch = 36 sts.

Border of center (WS)

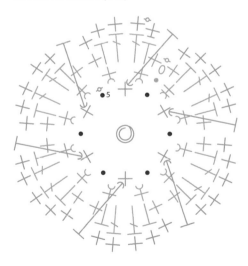

- Yarn A
- Yarn B
- Yarn C
- Yarn D

Second flower layer

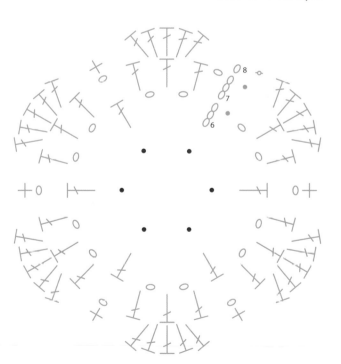

THIRD FLOWER LAYER

Rnd 9: Work behind second flower layer. With Yarn D, *1 sl st in an sc, ch 5, skip 5 dc, 1 sl st in next sc*; rep * to * 4 more times, ch 5, cut yarn, and end with 1 invisible sl st in the 1st ch = 6 ch loops.

Rnd 10: With Yarn B, work 1 incomplete standing around a ch loop, *[skip 1 sl st, 1 incomplete dc around next ch loop, dc2tog; around same ch loop, work dc2tog, 5 dc, dc2tog] and 1 incomplete dc*; rep * to * 4 more times, rep within brackets once more, cut yarn, and end with 1 invisible sl st in the 1st dc2tog = 48 dc.

Rnd 11: With Yarn A, work 1 standing sc in back loop only in any dc; sc in back loops only around, cut yarn, and end with 1 invisible sl st in back loop only in the standing sc = 48 sc.

Rnd 12: Beg rnd in an sc situated vertically in line with the center dc of a group of 5 dc on Rnd 10. With Yarn C, work 1 5-dc bobble (work the 1st as a standing dc) in this sc, *[2 dc in each of next 2 sc; 1 incomplete dc in next sc, skip 1 sc, 1 incomplete dc in next sc, dc2tog; 2 dc in each of next 2 sc], 1 5-dc bobble in next sc*; rep * to * 4 more times, rep within brackets once more, cut yarn, and end with 1 invisible sl st in the 1st bobble = 60 sts.

Rnd 13: Beg rnd 2 dc before a bobble. With Yarn A, work 1 standing sc in this dc, *[1 dc in back loop only in next dc of Rnd 10, skip 1 dc, 1 sc in next bobble, 1 dc in back loop only in next dc of Rnd 10, skip 1 dc, 1 sc in each of next 3 dc, 1 elongated sc in the next free sc of Rnd 10 (tighten this sc as much as possible)], 1 sc in each of next 3 dc*; rep * to * 4 more times, rep within brackets once more, 1 sc in each of last 2 dc, cut yarn, and end with 1 invisible sl st in the standing sc.

Rnd 14: With Yarn B, work 1 standing dc and 2 dc in same sc situated vertically in line with a bobble on Rnd 12, *[3 dc in next dc, 2 dc in next sc, 1 dc in next sc, 1 hdc in next sc, sc2tog in next 2 sc, 1 hdc in next st, 1 dc in next st, 2 dc in next st], 3 dc in next st*; rep * to * 4 more times, rep within brackets once more, cut yarn, and end with 1 invisible sl st in the standing dc = 90 sts.

Rnd 15: With Yarn A, work 1 standing sc in back loop only in any st; sc in back loops only around, cut yarn, and end with 1 invisible sl st in back loop only in the standing sc = 90 sc.

Rnd 16: Find an hdc preceding a dc2tog on Rnd 14. With Yarn D, work 1 standing dc in the sc situated vertically in line with this hdc, *[sc2tog in next 2 sc, 1 hdc in next sc, 1 dc in each of next 4 sc, 2 dc in each of next 3 sc, 1 dc in each of next 4 sc], 1 hdc in next sc*; rep * to * 4 more times, rep within brackets once more, cut yarn, and end with 1 invisible sl st in the standing dc = 102 sts.

Weave in ends. Block the work (see page 13), without pinning either the first flower layer or the last round of the third flower layer. Let dry in sunshine for multiple days, if possible.

Cut a circle of fabric about 24¾ in / 63 cm in diameter. Fold edges over and sew down, by machine or by hand, about ½ in / 1.5 cm from the fold to create a tube; insert a doubled length of sewing thread for a drawstring. Center the pillow form on WS. Pull on the thread so the fabric gathers around the pillow form, covering it fully, and then fasten off. Pin crocheted work to center of cushion, over where the fabric is gathered. Working from below, sew down with small stitches along Rnd 15, leaving Rnd 16 loose.

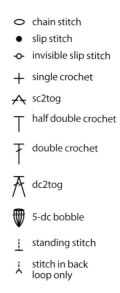

- ⬭ chain stitch
- ● slip stitch
- ⊶ invisible slip stitch
- + single crochet
- ⋀ sc2tog
- T half double crochet
- ⊤ double crochet
- ⋀ dc2tog
- ⬛ 5-dc bobble
- ⫶ standing stitch
- ⋀ stitch in back loop only

On Rnd 13 (Yarn A), stitches worked into
Rnd 10 are marked in black for clarity.

— Yarn A
— Yarn B
— Yarn C
— Yarn D

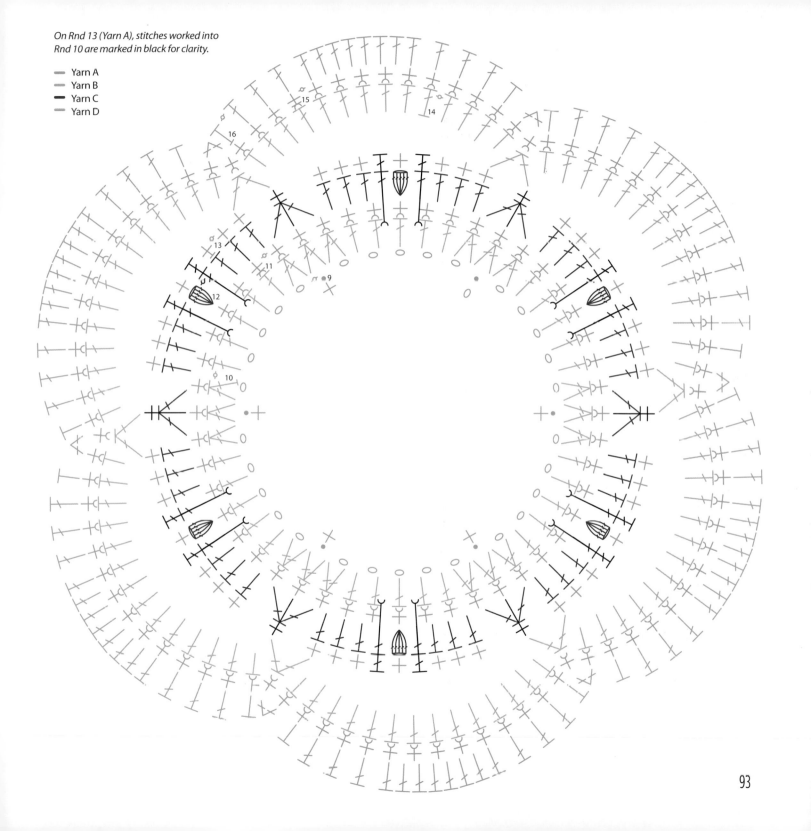

93

SUPPLIES AND YARN INFORMATION

DMC Corporation
10 Basin Drive, Suite 130
Kearny, NJ 07032
800-275-4117
www.dmc-usa.com

Webs – America's Yarn Store
75 Service Center Road
Northampton, MA 01060
800-367-9327
www.yarn.com
customerservice@yarn.com

LoveKnitting.com
www.loveknitting.com/us

If you are unable to obtain any of the yarn used in this book, it can be replaced with a yarn of a similar weight and composition. Please note, however, the finished projects may vary slightly from those shown, depending on the yarn used. Try www.yarnsub.com for suggestions.

For more information on selecting or substituting yarn, contact your local yarn shop or an online store; they are familiar with all types of yarns and would be happy to help you. Additionally, the online knitting community at Ravelry.com has forums where you can post questions about specific yarns.

Yarns come and go so quickly these days and there are so many beautiful yarns available.

ACKNOWLEDGMENTS

This book would never have seen the light of day without my parents, who helped me found PurPle Laines. I am forever grateful. Thank you to Isabelle Kessedjian, who put me in touch with Marylise Trioreau at my French publisher's office at Éditions Mango. Marylise believed in me and supported me through this project. Thank you also to Fabrice Besse and Sonia Roy for their superb photos and their willingness to work together to create the exact atmosphere I'd hoped for.

Thank you to Noël, my husband, for the unshakable confidence he has in me, for his support through hours of me crocheting while he drove, for putting up with having a light on right next to the television every night for me to crochet by. Thank you to Clarisse, who always finds the right words to encourage me. Thank you to Lili, who taught me how to crochet again at the corner of the bar at Estaminet, twenty-five years ago.

The editor thanks DMC Corporation for providing most of the yarn used to create the projects photographed in this book.

The stylist thanks Monoprix.

ABOUT THE AUTHOR

Marie-Line André, founder of PurPle Laines

Marie-Line began sewing, knitting, and crocheting when she was six years old. When she was in high school, she started making her own sweaters and other clothing, adopting a colorful vintage style. She also has always loved crocheting complex, delicate designs, and soon took up Irish lacework—a technique requiring patience, steady hands, and intense attention to detail.

In 2013, after working for several years as a teacher, Marie-Line changed tracks and began her small business with a shop, PurPle Laines, and the accompanying blog, Le Blog PurPle. She loves offering especially striking color combinations to her clients.

In 2014, she joined the editorial team of the French magazine *Passion Tricot* [Knitting Passion] and now divides her time between her family, her store, and the magazine. In the evenings, she knits and crochets, always with the loveliest colors she can find, in an attempt to make every day a little bit beautiful.

www.purple-laines.com
www.leblogpurple.com